48-Hour
Country
Quilts

❖

Signature Quilt

48-Hour Country Quilts

Fran Roen

Sterling Publishing Co., Inc. New York

This book is dedicated to my very best friend, Jah; my wonderful husband, Ron; my beautiful children, Cressenda, Carry, Caleb, Charlyn, Clint, and Charlie; and, of course, the first quilter I knew, my mother, Fran Bush.

In-House Editor Jeanette Green
Copyedited by Laurel Ornitz
Photography by Billy Robin McFarland
Illustrated by Fran Roen

Library of Congress Cataloging-in-Publication Data

Roen, Fran.
    48-hour country quilts / by Fran Roen ; illustrations by Fran
Roen.
        p.   cm.
    Includes index.
    ISBN 0-8069-0386-4
    1. Machine quilting—Patterns.   2. Patchwork—Patterns.
I. Title.   II. Title: Forty eight-hour country quilts.
TT835.R585   1993
746.9′7—dc20   93-5088
                                                                    CIP

            2   4   6   8   10   9   7   5   3

Published in 1993 by Sterling Publishing Company, Inc.
387 Park Avenue South, New York, N.Y. 10016
© 1993 by Fran Roen
Distributed in Canada by Sterling Publishing
℅ Canadian Manda Group, P.O. Box 920, Station U
Toronto, Ontario, Canada M8Z 5P9
Distributed in Great Britain and Europe by Cassell PLC
Villiers House, 41/47 Strand, London WC2N 5JE, England
Distributed in Australia by Capricorn Link Ltd.
P.O. Box 665, Lane Cove, NSW 2066
Manufactured in the United States of America
All rights reserved

Sterling ISBN 0-8069-0386-4

Contents

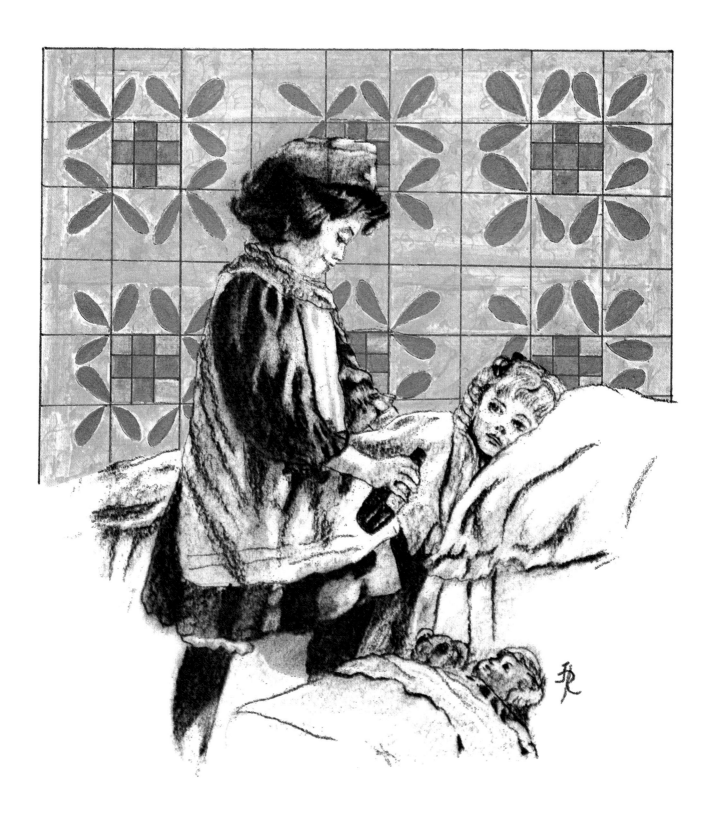

Honeybee (*see p. 29*)

Introduction

Quilting has always been a wonderful way to express artistic inclinations and talent, work out frustrations, and even help handle grief.

Quilting has never been just a pastime for the little old lady down the street. Throughout history, quilters have been men, women, and children. In some cultures, if you were old enough to handle a needle, you were old enough to learn to quilt.

A quilter's mind is generally as sharp as his or her needle. Creativity and inventiveness are also called for in the process. You may not think you have these qualities, but by starting on one of the easy patterns for speed quilts in this book you'll soon discover many unknown talents and abilities just waiting to be tapped.

Tools and Materials

Backing

The backing is the fabric on the underside of your quilt, usually made of 6 to 7 yards of 100-percent cotton muslin. Some people like to use a sheet for the back. Should you do this, remove all seams and wash the sheet before using it. Always buy the sheet one size larger than the quilt you plan to make.

Batting

This is the filling that goes between your pieced top and the backing. There are generally two types of batting: cotton and polyester. *Cotton*, the traditional batting, is very nice to work with but not readily available. *Polyester* is equally nice to work with, readily available, and comes in many different styles.

There are also *bonded* and *unbonded* battings and a wide range of lofts, from low to ultra-high. Other types of batting, like fleece, are also available, but for the projects in this book, cotton or polyester battings are the best and most often used.

Have you ever taken your polyester batting out of its plastic bag only to find that you couldn't get it back in? That's because, as soon as you take it out of the bag, the batting begins to fill with air; this is called *breathing*. When you open the bag, you'll notice that there may appear to be both thin and clumpy areas. What you need to do is lay the batting out open on a table overnight to allow it to breathe. If you don't have the space or time, put the batting in the dryer on the delicate cycle for a few minutes.

Colors

I like to select a large-print piece with a good color scheme and build from it. I pick out colors from the large print to use in the rest of the quilt. Even if I don't use the large print in the quilt, I'll know that the colors go together. You need to be careful when using large prints in quilts because more than one may make the quilt appear too busy. Large prints work best in large areas.

Sometimes I use a color wheel that I bought at an art supply store. But, no matter how you choose your colors, always play the light colors against the dark or vice versa. For example, if you want a flower to stand out, you could use dark petals against a light background. Medium colors against medium colors will always blend in, even if the colors are different. Light against dark or dark against light always creates a striking effect in a quilt.

Fabric

I prefer to use 100-percent cotton for my quilts; however, you can use almost any type of fabric for quilting as long as all your choices have the same weight and fabric content.

All fabrics should be prewashed. Check to make sure all your fabric is color-fast. If you find you have a bleeder, fill your washing machine to its lowest level with cold water and add a mixture of 1¼ cups of white vinegar and ½ cup of salt (this mixture will set colors nine times out of ten). I allow the fabric to soak for at least 4 hours, but overnight, when possible, is better. If the fabric still bleeds after this, then label your finished quilt "dry clean only." I prefer to simply choose a different fabric; I want washable quilts.

Iron

Pressing is a must. When pressed, your blocks will be kept flat, without puckers or unwanted folds. Pressing also helps to keep the blocks square. Remember, there is a difference between pressing and ironing. *Pressing* is, just as the word implies, pressing the weight of the iron down on your fabric to achieve an even heat flow. *Ironing* is done with a back-and-forth movement of the iron. With the small pieces of fabric used in quilting, ironing may cause them to roll.

Needles

Always keep a good supply of needles on hand. If your sewing machine needle is bent or rough, replace it. Don't wait until it breaks. Generally, I use sewing machine needle sizes 12 or 14. For hand quilting, I use "betweens," needle sizes 7 to 12. For tying your quilt, you will need a large-eyed needle to use with a good-quality yarn or embroidery floss.

Oil

Make sure you have the right kind of sewing-machine oil on hand and use it often.

Pressing Surface

Use an ironing board or an ironing pad. To make your own ironing pad, buy an ironing board cover, measure about 2 feet up from the bottom of the cover, and cut it across. Remove all elastic and square it off. Cut a piece of batting and backing the same size, and then sew them together. Now you can press anywhere on the pad without worrying about damaging the surface, such as your kitchen table, beneath the pad.

Quilting Pins

Extra-long quilting pins are the most practical type to use for these projects. Also have a number of large safety pins on hand if you plan to hand- or machine-quilt your project. It will take about twenty to twenty-four dozen pins to piece together a king-size quilt.

Rotary Cutter and Mat

After the sewing machine, these tools are the most important aids in speed quilting. Rotary cutters are generally sold in two sizes: small and large. Mats come in many sizes. Without a mat or cutting board under your fabric, your work surface will become badly scored and your blade will dull quickly.

Ruler

The best ruler to use for quilt making is an *acrylic quilter's ruler*, but these can be expensive. However, most of the patterns in this book require 2½-inch strips, so you could go to your local hardware store and have a piece of Plexiglas cut to measure 2½ × 27 inches. (Make sure that the piece measures 2½ inches across, down its full length, before leaving the store.) Plexiglas is a very affordable alternative; my piece cost less than two dollars.

Child's Pineapple (see p. 37)

Victorian Lap Quilt (*see p.* 49)

Seam Ripper

We are all imperfect; this tool allows us to get rid of our mistakes quickly and cleanly. Mine is always nearby.

Scissors

It's a good idea to keep one pair of sharp scissors next to your sewing machine and another pair on your work surface. That way, you can cut off small threads right away instead of having to go back to cut them later.

Sewing Machine

Any well-running sewing machine will do. If you also have a serger, I would suggest using it, but you can get along just fine without one. Make sure that your sewing machine is well-oiled, the thread tension is on the correct setting, and everything is running smoothly. Nothing seems to stop a project as fast as a poorly operating machine. Unfortunately, most of those stopped projects never seem to get picked up again.

Thread

Cotton thread is best, but it is often hard to come by. Cotton-covered polyester thread is much more readily available and works just as well. Whatever you choose, remember that you want your quilt to last, so select the best quality of thread that you can afford.

Speed Techniques

Using a Rotary Cutter

Lay your cutting mat or board on your work surface. Then lay down your first piece of fabric so that the grain is vertical to you. (Cut all strips with the grain, or from selvage to selvage.) Now lay down the rest of your fabrics, one on top of the other, with all grains aligned. Make sure all fabric is smooth. The rotary cutter can cut through as much as six layers of fabric at one time. Remember that the more fabric you cut at one time, the greater the pressure you'll need to apply to the cutter. (A helpful hint: The more vertical the rotary cutter, the less pressure you'll need.) If you are right-handed, place all your fabric to the right. Then start cutting at the far left, and work towards the right. If you are left-handed, do the opposite.

Before cutting your first strip, even off the edges so that they all line up. Then, using your ruler, measure in 2½ inches from the edge, press down firmly on your ruler, and run your rotary cutter along the ruler's edge. If you did not cut through all layers, go back with your scissors and finish. As you become more experienced, you will learn to apply just the right amount of pressure to avoid this problem.

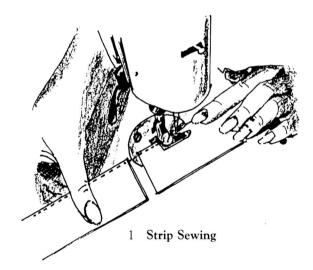

1   Strip Sewing

Strip Sewing

Choose a pair of strips in complementary colors. With right sides together, sew the length of the strips without cutting them loose from the sewing machine. Simply butt in the next set of strips (see 1), and continue with the other pairs until they are all sewn together. This real time-saver is also known as *chain stitching.*

Speed Appliqué

I prefer this method because I don't like having to work around a lot of small raw edges and straight pins.

Lay down fusible interfacing with the glue side faceup. Top with your fabric facedown. Cut out your pattern shape. Stitch within ¼ inch of the edge, through both the fabric and interfacing, all the way around. Clip any curved edges. Cut an X in the interfacing, pull the fabric through, and smooth out the edges.

You now have the right side of the fabric on the top, with the glue side of the interfacing on the bottom. Lay on the background fabric; apply a warm iron. It will now stay in place for you to stitch around. No pins, no sliding, and no raw edges.

Half-Square Triangles

To make a half-square triangle (also called a *triangle-square*), start by creating a grid on the back of your darkest fabric. If your finished square is supposed to measure 4 inches, then your grid should consist of 5-inch squares. After you have drawn the grid, draw a diagonal line through each of the squares (see 2).

Next, lay your fabric facedown on a piece of fabric of a complementary color. Now you are ready to sew the triangles. Line up the fabric on your sewing machine so that the needle is ½ inch from the first diagonal line, and sew the length of the line. But make sure that you pick up the needle each time you come to the point of another triangle. Do not sew through it. When you have finished the first line, turn your fabric 180 degrees and sew along the other side of the first diagonal line, making sure to leave a ½-inch seam allowance. When you have sewn along both sides of all the diagonal lines, then cut along the outlines of the squares and along the diagonal lines. Your triangles are now ready to be pressed and used in your pattern.

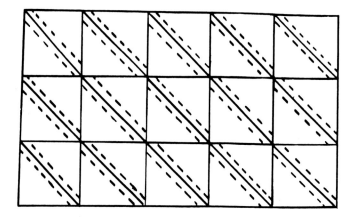

2 Half-Square Triangles

Double Half-Square Triangles

There are many ways to sew a double half-square triangle. I happen to like this method best. (Each pattern in this book that uses the double half-square triangle will give the sizes of rectangles needed.) Using two rectangles of the same size, right sides together, finger-press the corners into the center (see 3). Start to sew from the center of the top to the lower bottom, sewing diagonally (see 4). Sew the opposite side in the same way. Trim off excess fabric within ¼ inch of the stitch line, on both sides (see 5). Now cut up the center of only one triangle. Press open.

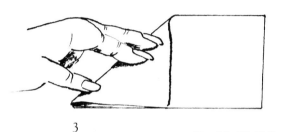 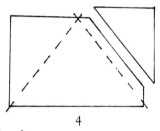 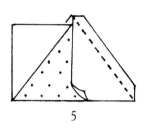

3   **Double Half-Square Triangles**   4   5

Backing the Quilt

I have three favorite ways of backing my quilts. The first is *bias binding*. For this method, use a fabric that complements the quilt top.

To make your own bias seam strip, lay the fabric on a flat surface and find the 45-degree bias line (see 6). Trim off the bottom and cut on the diagonal (see 7). Sew it back together, as shown in 8. Iron flat. Your bias strip should be six times wider than you want the finished binding. (For example, if you want a 1-inch binding around your quilt, cut a 6-inch strip.) For cutting, see 9. Fold it in half and iron flat. Pin the binding around your quilt with the raw edge towards the outside of your quilt. If your binding is to be 1 inch, then your seam allowance must be 1 inch. Sew on the binding all the way around to the other side and stitch it into place.

A second method involves *laying the backing wrong side up*. Then lay the batting on top of it and the quilt on top of that. Trim the batting to fit the quilt, and make the backing 2 inches larger around the quilt's perimeter. Fold the back over both the batting and the quilt top, and form a ¼-inch hem from the backing material. Sew through all layers all the way around.

The third technique is the *pillowcase method*. This is fast and easy. To

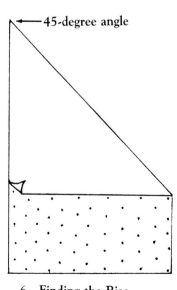

6   **Finding the Bias**

15

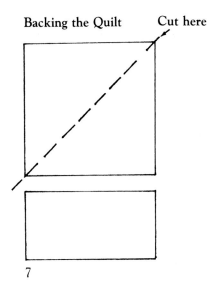

Backing the Quilt — Cut here

7

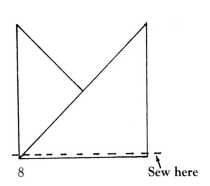

begin, lay your batting down on the floor, your backing faceup, and then your quilt facedown on top of the backing. Pin and sew the edges of all three layers, with your machine set for ten to twelve stitches per inch. Sew all the way around, except for a 3-foot opening on one side. Cut your quilt free from the machine, and trim the batting close to the stitching. Roll the corners and sides tightly towards the opening, and pull the whole quilt through the hole. Flatten your quilt and slip-stitch the opening. The fabric needed for the backing is generally 6 to 7 yards.

Adding Borders

In this book, all of the quilt patterns have Amish borders and most of the patterns require three. To adjust the size of your quilt, you may wish to add or subtract borders.

Here is an example of what the pattern may require and how to handle it:

First border	eight strips 3 × 45 inches
Second border	eight strips 4 × 45 inches
Third border	eight strips 5 × 45 inches

For the first border, pair off your strips and sew them together on their short ends. Sew the first border to the sides, next on the top, and then on the bottom. Attach the second border in the same order. Then do the same with the third border.

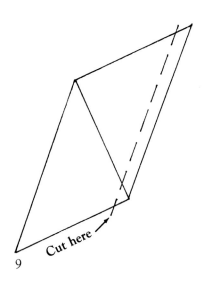

8 — Sew here

9 — Cut here

Machine Tying

Mark your quilt top with a chalk pencil. If your are using cotton batting, mark every 2 or 3 inches. If you are using polyester batting, mark every 5 or 6 inches. Always begin marking in the center of your quilt, and work on a flat surface. Pin around your marks, which are called *tie points*.

When you have finished marking and pinning your quilt, roll the sides of the quilt in towards the middle. This will make it easier to maneuver the quilt. Be sure to lower your machine's feed dogs, and use your regular zigzag stitch. Start sewing at the center of your quilt, and work towards the edges. Pull both ends of a piece of yarn through the first tie point, and make a knot or bow. Then lower the presser foot and zigzag over the center of the tie. This is called *bar tacking*. Move to your next tie point, and make another yarn knot or bow and bar-tack. When you are finished, clip loose threads and remove all pins.

Diagonal Quilting by Machine

We'll be marking fabric on the bias (see 6). If the project is small, marks should be 2 inches apart. If the project is large, marks should be 5 or 6 inches apart. To find the bias of your quilt, lay it on a flat surface so that the grain is vertical to you. Next, fold the right corner over towards the left until the grain of the folded piece is perpendicular to the grain of the fabric underneath. Press very lightly along the fold to create a guideline. Then open the fold, take a ruler, and mark each line with chalk or a pencil at the appropriate distance. (An erasable pen may leave a line that we cannot see, but eventually that "erased" line may become yellow. I learned this the hard way!) See 10.

Row 3

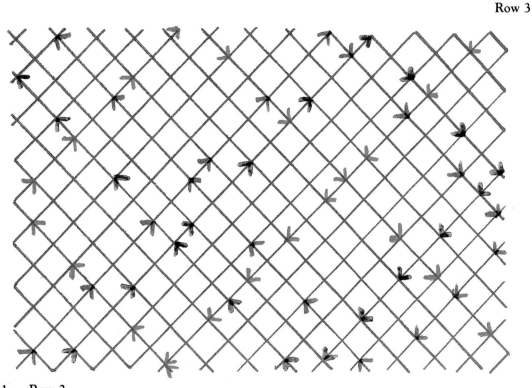

Row 1   Row 2

10 **Diagonal Quilting by Machine**

Hanging Your Quilt

To make a casing for your quilt, cut a piece of cotton 6 inches times the finished width of your quilt minus 2 inches. (I put two casings on my quilts, one on the top and one on the bottom. See Helpful Hints to see why.) Hem both short ends. Center the casing on the back of your quilt, and slip-stitch it in place.

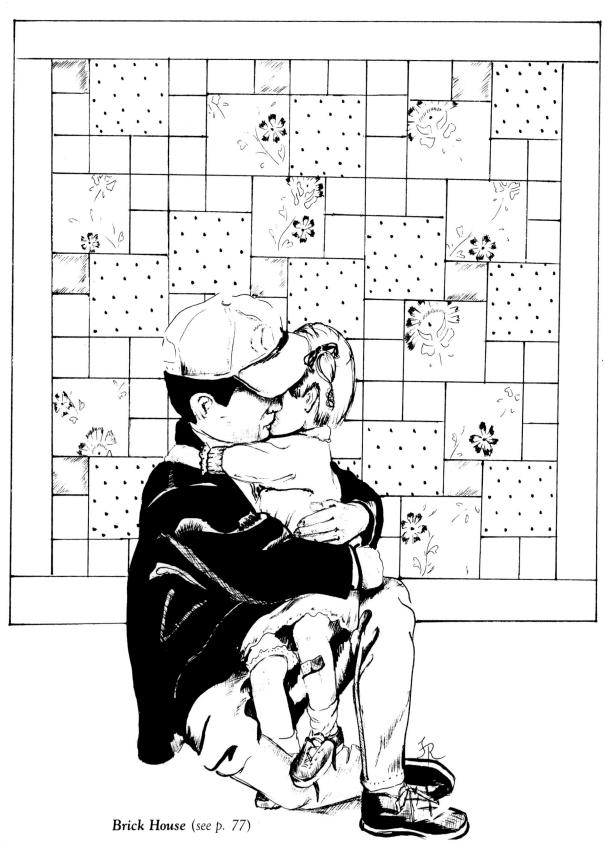

Brick House (*see p. 77*)

Helpful Hints

- Always prewash your fabrics.
- Fraying is usually a problem when prewashing fabric. To prevent this, snip off a corner at a 45-degree angle on both ends of the fabric, not each corner. Make the cut only about 1 to 1½ inches.
- Set your machine for ten to twelve stitches per inch.
- When sewing, use a ¼-inch seam allowance.
- For a lovely finished quilt, take time to cut, sew, and press your pieces accurately.
- When joining two pieces that already have seams, sew seams in opposite directions to avoid bulk.
- When pressing seams, press them towards the darkest fabric to avoid a shadow behind light colors.
- Do you need a ruffle for a pillow and hate to gather? Zigzag over a piece of twine or crochet thread on the fabric you want ruffled; then pull the twine gently. It will gather neatly.
- Label quilts with your name and date. Here are some ways to do this: Use a permanent marker, cross-stitch the label on the quilt with waste canvas, or take a piece of white cotton fabric and type the information and then slip-stitch the label into place.
- To keep the knots in place when tying your quilt, apply a drop of waterproof glue.
- When hanging a quilt on a wall, rotate it every six months or so. First hang the quilt from the top, then from the bottom, since the constant pull on the threads can cause them to break.
- Make a heavy-duty template out of a plastic lid from a soft-margarine container. If it is slippery, rough up the back a little with sandpaper.
- I hate rethreading my sewing machine every time I run out of thread. So I tie the end of the old thread to the end of the new thread. Then I continue to sew. As I'm sewing, the new thread will run through the machine, being pulled along by the old thread. When the knot arrives at the needle, I cut it off, thread my needle, and continue sewing.
- Never use nails or tacks to hang quilts. Why put holes in them? And eventually they will sag, making the holes even bigger.
- When storing your quilt, never keep it in plastic. Since plastic doesn't breathe, it allows moisture and insects to keep your quilt company until you air it out again.
- Air your quilt out and refold it in different directions every three or four months. Place it in a box lined with cotton sheets.

Framed Quilt

1 Framed Quilt

Framed quilts were very popular both to make and give as gifts between the 1840s and 1890s.

YARDAGE

Center panel	14 × 14 inches
Fabric A	1½ yards
Fabric B	⅓ yard
Fabric C	¼ yard
Fabric D	1½ yards
Fabric E	2 yards
Fabric F	½ yard
Fabric G	3¾ yards

CUTTING

Fabric A	twelve strips 2½ × 45 inches (cut into 5- × -2½-inch rectangles, ninety-six total)
Fabric A, first inside border	two strips 3½ × 45 inches
Fabric B, second inside border	four strips 2 × 45 inches
Fabric D	four strips 3¾ × 45 inches
Fabric D, first outside border	eight strips 4 × 45 inches
Fabric E	four strips 3¾ × 45 inches
Fabric E, second outside border	eight strips 5 × 45 inches
Fabric F	two strips 7 × 45 inches (cut into 7- × -7-inch squares, eight total)
Fabric G, third inside border	four strips 4 × 45 inches
Fabric G	seven strips 2 × 45 inches
Fabric G, third outside border	eight strips 6 × 45 inches
Fabric G	twelve strips 2½ × 45 inches (cut into 5- × -2½-inch rectangles, ninety-six total)

SEWING DIRECTIONS

Size: 86 × 86 inches

1. Take the remainder of fabric A, and, using fabric C, draft six-

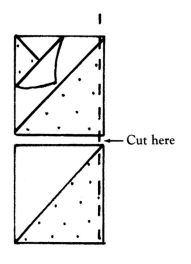

— Cut here

teen 3-by-3-inch squares. Follow the directions in the Speed Techniques section for "Half-square triangles." Sew and cut. When done, you'll have a total of thirty-two triangle-squares. Press.

2. Sew six triangle-squares together (see 1–1), and attach to one of the sides of the center panel. Repeat for the opposite side.

Sew six triangle-squares together, as shown in 1–2. Repeat a second time; then attach one square at each end, as shown in 1–3 and 1–4.

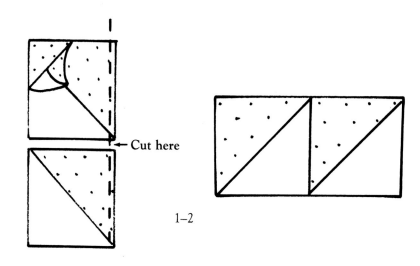

— Cut here

1–2

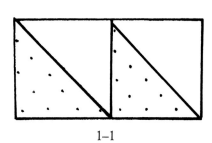

1–1

3. Press and attach to the top and bottom of the center panel (see photo). Sew the first inside border on. (See "Adding borders" in Speed Techniques.) Sew the second inside border on.

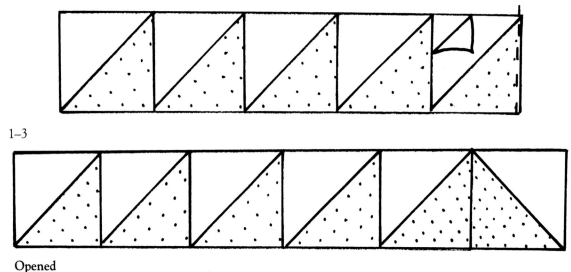

1–3

Opened

4. Place a 3¾-inch fabric D strip faceup on your sewing machine. Top with a 3¾-inch fabric E strip facedown. Sew the length. Repeat for a total of four times.

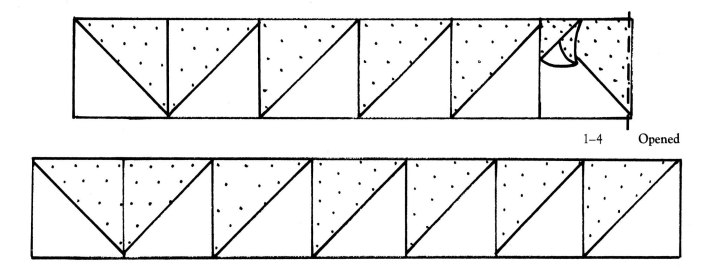

1-4   **Opened**

Measure down 7 inches and cut; you'll need sixteen pieces.

Sew four pieces together, alternating colors to form a brick pattern. Repeat three more times. Attach one brick section to each of the sides of the center piece.

Sew a 7-inch square from fabric F to each end of the two remaining brick sections, and attach to the top and bottom of the center piece.

5. Attach the third inside border, and set the center piece aside.

6. Using the 5-inch rectangles from fabrics A and G, follow the directions for making double half-square triangles in Speed Techniques. Make a total of ninety-six.

7. Place a 2-by-45-inch fabric G strip faceup on your sewing machine. Lay a double half-square triangle block facedown and sew. Butt in until all have been attached to a 2-inch strip; cut apart (see 1–5). Place a 2-by-45-inch fabric G strip faceup on your sewing machine. Lay a double half-square triangle block facedown, with the newly attached spacer to the left. Sew; butt in until four have been sewn on. Cut apart. These will be the beginners for each of the four rolls.

8. Sew on beginners to seven double half-square triangle blocks. Repeat for a total of four times.

9. Sew one to each side of the center piece. With the remaining two, add a 7-by-7-inch square from fabric F to each end. (Check to make sure this will fit. If your seams are too large or too small, some adjustment may be needed.) Sew to the top and bottom.

10. Add three outside borders, consisting of fabrics D, E, and F, in that order. (Refer to "Adding Borders" in Speed Techniques.) Finish the quilt as you like.

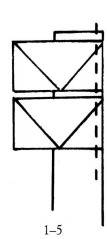

1-5

Wedding Ring or Georgetown Circle

2 Wedding Ring *or* Georgetown Circle

This quilt pattern first appeared between 1785 and 1800, when New York was the United States capital. Since then, the capital was moved from New York to Washington, D.C. For many years, the name Georgetown Circle was the preferred name for this pattern. Now, most quilters call it the Wedding Ring.

YARDAGE

Fabric A	¾ yard
Fabric B	1¾ yards
Fabric C	½ yard
Fabric D	⅔ yard
Fabric E	2 yards
Fabric E, first border	1 yard
Fabric B, second border	1 yard
Fabric E, third border	1½ yards

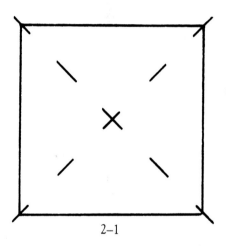

2–1

CUTTING

Fabric A	five strips 4½ × 45 inches (cut into 4½- × -4½-inch squares, twenty-four total)
Fabric B	five strips 5 × 45 inches (cut into 5- × -5-inch squares, twenty-four total; then cut on the diagonals, as shown in 2–1)
Fabric C	six strips 2½ × 45 inches
Fabric D	nine strips 2½ × 45 inches
Fabric E	six strips 2½ × 45 inches
Fabric E	five strips 3½ × 45 inches
Fabric E	twelve strips 12 × 12 inches
Fabric E, first border	eight strips 3 × 45 inches
Fabric B, second border	eight strips 4 × 45 inches
Fabric E, third border	eight strips 6 × 45 inches

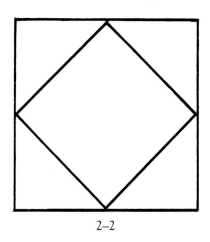

2–2

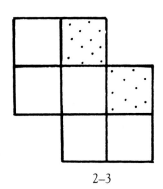

2–3

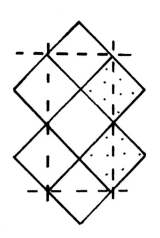

SEWING DIRECTIONS

Size: 68 × 91 inches

1. Sew fabric A squares and fabric B triangles, as shown in 2–2. Press flat and square off if needed. Your square should be 6-by-6 inches. Set aside.

2. Sew the length of a 2½-inch fabric C strip with a 2½-inch fabric D strip. Repeat for a total of 6 times. These will be called "sewn-strips A." Press flat and set aside.

We'll make "sewn-strips B" by sewing a 2½-inch fabric C strip to a 2½-inch fabric D strip and then sewing these to a 2½-inch fabric E strip. Repeat for a total of six times. Press and set aside.

Sew a 2½-inch fabric D strip to a 2½-inch fabric E strip; repeat for a total of six times. Press flat and set aside. These are the "sewn-strips C."

3. On your cutting surface, stack "sewn-strips A, B, and C," one of each. Measure down 2½ inches and cut. Cut all the way down your strips, and keep them in this order because this is the order in which they will be sewn. (You should get a total of sixteen cuts per strip.) Repeat until all sewn strips are cut.

4. Sew your blocks together, as shown in 2–3, matching seams carefully. Repeat until all are sewn. Press flat.

5. Cut your pieces from Step 4, as shown in 2–4.

6. Place a block from Step 1 faceup on your sewing machine, and attach a piece from Step 5 facedown with the fabric C triangle towards the square. Sew. Repeat for a total of twelve times. Attach one on the opposite side. Press flat and set aside.

7. Place a 3½-inch strip faceup on your sewing machine. Lay a piece from Step 5 facedown, and sew the shortest end to the strip. Continue butting triangle pieces until all are attached to a strip. Cut apart, as shown in 2–5.

Now attach the opposite side of your triangle piece to a 3½-inch strip. Butt in until all are again attached to a 3½-inch strip. Cut apart, as shown in 2–6, and press flat.

8. The pieces from Step 7 are the top and bottom to the pieces in Step 6. Sew them together, referring to 2–7 when needed. This is your finished block.

9. Your top with be six rolls deep—each roll having four blocks, two pieced alternating with two solids. Attach borders one and two, as directed in "Adding Borders" in the Speed Techniques section.

10. Attach a square from Step 1 to the end of four of your third border pieces. Measure the side of your top. Cut the excess from the strip, making sure to allow for seam allowance. Sew the short ends of the border piece. Attach to the side as you would any border. Make sure that the squares are in the corners.

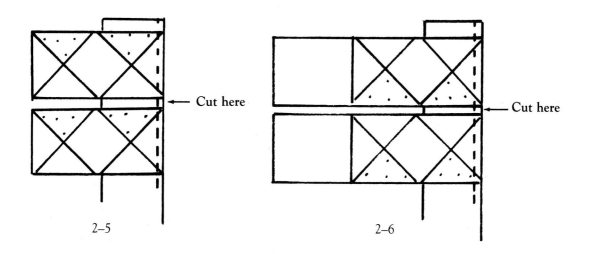

2–5   2–6

11. Sew two squares together from Step 1; repeat for a total of four times. Attach these to the ends of four of your third border pieces. Measure the top and bottom; cut off excess and attach as any border.

Finish your quilt as you wish (remember, tying quilts has been around for more than 250 years).

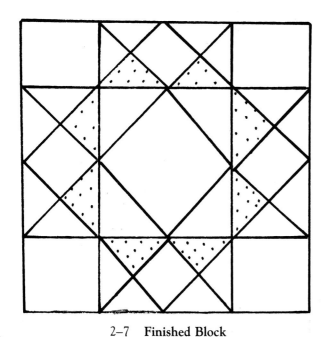

2–7   **Finished Block**

Honeybee

3　Honeybee

This quilt is a pleasing balance of pieced work and appliqué. The pattern easily lives up to its name. The nine-block section has four honeybees ready to land on a flower.

YARDAGE

Fabric A, main color	4½ yards
Fabric B, honeybees	1¾ yards
Fabric C, center of the flower	¼ yard
Fabric D, flower	½ yard
Fabric E, flower	½ yard
Fusible interfacing	2 yards
First border	¾ yard
Second border	1 yard
Third border	1½ yards

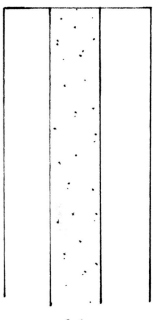

3–1

CUTTING

Fabric A	twenty strips 7¼ × 45 inches
Fabric C	one strip 3 × 45 inches
Fabric D	four strips 3 × 45 inches
Fabric E	four strips 3 × 45 inches
First border	eight strips 3 × 45 inches
Second border	eight strips 4 × 45 inches
Third border	eight strips 5 × 45 inches

SEWING DIRECTIONS

Size: 86 × 108 inches

　1. Before beginning, review "Speed Appliqué" in the Speed Techniques section.

　2. From fabric B and the fusible interfacing, cut 144 honeybees. Use the pattern piece provided (3–8). Sew and turn, as directed in "Speed Appliqué." Set aside.

　3. Lay a fabric E strip faceup on your sewing machine, lay a fabric D strip facedown, and sew them lengthwise. Now open up and sew a fabric E strip to the other side of fabric D (see 3–1). Sew two of these sets. Press and set aside.

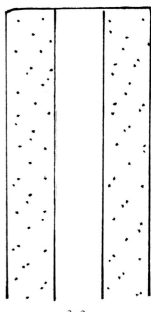

3–2

4. Now sew only one set in the following order: D, C, D (see 3–2). Press.

Measure down 3 inches on one of the sets and cut. (For speed, carefully stack your sewn sheets one on top of the other; then measure and cut.) Repeat this step with the rest of the strip and with all the others. Sew the sections together to form a nine-block square (see 3–3). This pattern requires twelve nine-block squares. (Save any leftovers for a sampler or baby quilt.)

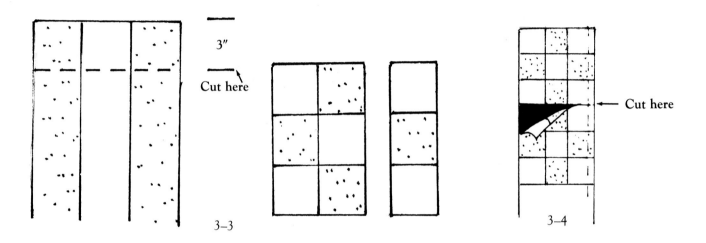

3–3

3–4

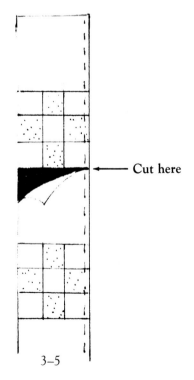

3–5

5. Lay a 7½-inch fabric A strip faceup on your sewing machine, and begin sewing the nine-block squares onto it; remember to place them facedown on the strip. Continue sewing until you have attached all twelve of your nine-block squares. Cut apart your blocks, as shown in 3–4.

6. Take another fabric A strip and lay it faceup on your sewing machine. Then take one of your newly sewn blocks and lay it facedown, lengthwise, on the strip. With the newly attached fabric A to the top, butt in the next block and sew in the same manner. Do the same with the rest of your nine blocks, adding strips as necessary. Cut apart, as shown in 3–5.

7. Lay another fabric A strip faceup on your sewing machine, and lay a block facedown on top of it. Again, make sure that the newly attached fabric A strip is at the top of the block. See 3–6.

8. Follow the same sewing steps until you have completed all the blocks. Cut where indicated in 3–6.

9. Place a fabric A strip faceup on your sewing machine, and lay a block facedown on top of it. Make sure that the newly attached fabric A strip is at the top of the block. Your finished block should look like the one shown in 3–7.

10. Now it's time to work with the honeybees that were made at the beginning of the project. Refer to the photo for placement. Press in place and stitch around the bees.

11. Sew your finished blocks together. Each quilt top will consist of four rows, each containing three blocks.

12. Sew borders on, as directed in "Adding Borders" in Speed Techniques. Finish the quilt using whatever method you prefer.

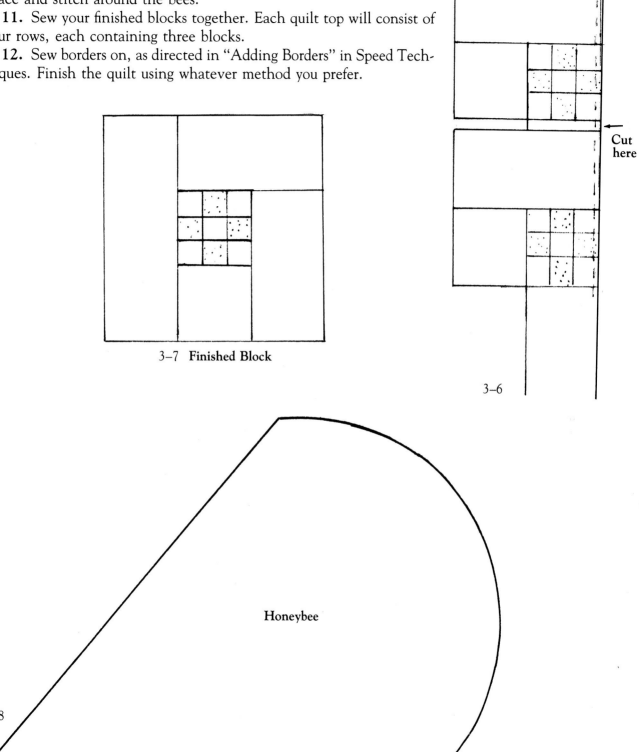

3–7 **Finished Block**

Cut here

3–6

Honeybee

3–8

Butterfly Quilt

4   Butterfly Quilt

This Butterfly Quilt is a good example of an appliquéd quilt. Appliquéd quilts are the oldest type of quilt. They are generally made on an all-white or off-white background.

YARDAGE

Fabric A, background	3 yards
Fabric B, upper wing	½ yard
Fabric C, lower wing	¼ yard
Fabric D, body	½ yard
Fusible interfacing	3 yards
First border	¾ yard
Second border	1 yard
Third border	1½ yards

CUTTING

Fabric A	twenty-five 12- × -12-inch squares
Fabric B, upper wing	twenty-six pieces cut from pattern (reverse half)
Upper-wing interfacing	twenty-six pieces cut from pattern (reverse half)
Fabric C, lower wing	twenty-six pieces cut from pattern (reverse half)
Lower-wing interfacing	twenty-six pieces cut from pattern (reverse half)
Fabric D, bodies	thirteen pieces cut from pattern
Bodies, interfacing	thirteen pieces cut from pattern
First border	eight strips 3 × 45 inches
Second border	eight strips 4 × 45 inches
Third border	eight strips 5 × 45 inches

SEWING DIRECTIONS

Size: 65 × 65 inches

1. Cut all the butterfly pattern pieces along with the interfacing. Then follow the directions for "Speed Appliqué" in the Speed Techniques section.

2. Press one of your 12-by-12-inch squares flat; then fold it in half,

then in quarters. This will allow you find the center. Using the fold line as a guide, lay two upper wings down on either side of the vertical fold line. Lay the lower wing in place, making sure to tuck the edge of the top under the upper wing (see 4–1). Press. Flip over and press the underside to make sure it is firmly attached. Repeat for a total of five times. Lay the body in the center; make sure to cover all the edges. Press it in place.

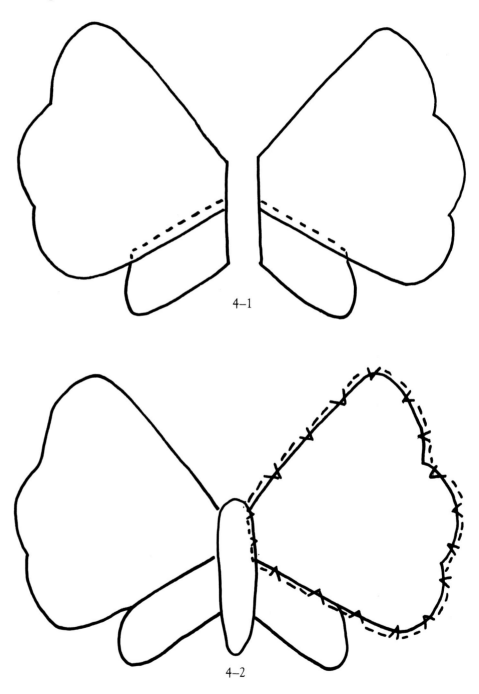

4–1

4–2

3. Using fourteen stitches per inch, stitch the butterfly on with the stitch as shown in 4–2 or with a zigzag stitch. Repeat for a total of five times.

4. Press one of your 12-by-12-inch squares flat, then on the diagonal, and fold again on the diagonal. Repeat for a total of eight times. Apply the butterfly as directed in Steps 2 and 3, only on the diagonal.

Sew your blocks as shown in the photo.

5. Attach borders as instructed in "Adding Borders" in Speed Techniques.

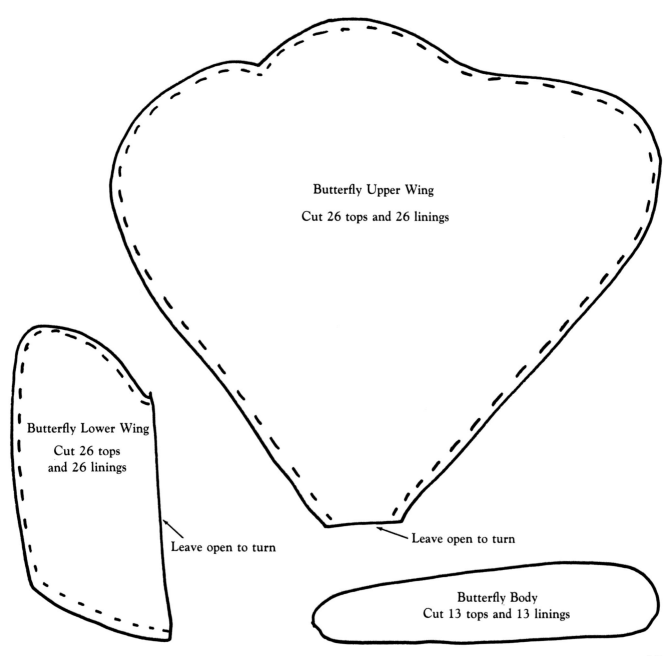

Butterfly Upper Wing

Cut 26 tops and 26 linings

Butterfly Lower Wing

Cut 26 tops
and 26 linings

Leave open to turn

Leave open to turn

Butterfly Body
Cut 13 tops and 13 linings

Child's Pineapple

5 Child's Pineapple

This pattern is similar to the Log Cabin pattern that originated in the United States. There was no room to set up a quilting loom in the covered wagons, so women would complete a quilt one block at a time and then piece the blocks together later. The Log Cabin pattern and its variations are block patterns that still enjoy worldwide popularity.

YARDAGE

Fabric A	¼ yard
Fabric B	1¼ yards
Fabric C	1¼ yards
Fabric D	1¼ yards
Fabric E	1¼ yards
First border	¾ yard
Second border	1 yard
Third border	1½ yards

CUTTING

Fabric A	three strips 5 × 45 inches (cut into 5-×-5-inch squares, twenty total)
Fabric B	sixteen strips 2½ × 45 inches
Fabric C	sixteen strips 2½ × 45 inches
Fabric D	sixteen strips 2½ × 45 inches
Fabric E	seven strips 5¾ × 45 inches (cut into forty 5¾-×-5¾-inch squares, then cut on the diagonal for a total of eighty triangles)
First border	eight strips 3 × 45 inches
Second border	eight strips 4 × 45 inches
Third border	eight strips 5 × 45 inches

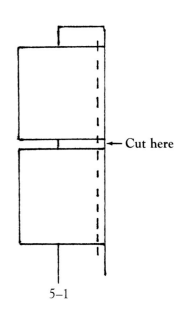

← Cut here

5–1

SEWING DIRECTIONS

Size: 70 × 82 inches

1. Place a fabric B strip faceup on your sewing machine. Lay a fabric A block facedown, and sew the length of your strip, butting in new

blocks. Continue until all blocks have been added to a strip. Cut as shown in 5–1.

2. Continue sewing in this fashion until all four sides have a fabric B strip added to them. Press and cut, as shown in 5–2.

The cut is made at a 45-degree angle. Cut the opposite corners first, and sew to a fabric C strip, as shown in 5–3. Remember that this cut is made on the bias, so be careful not to stretch the fabric when sewing.

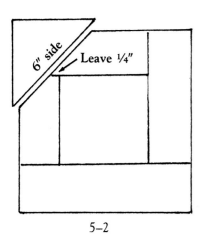

5–2

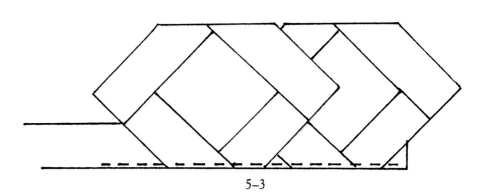

5–3

3. Cut the opposite corners and sew these to a fabric C strip. (By not cutting all the corners first, you may avoid getting confused.)

For cutting directions, see 5–4.

See 5–5 for how the block should look with the fabric C strip on all four corners. Press.

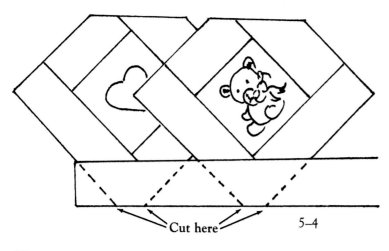

5–4

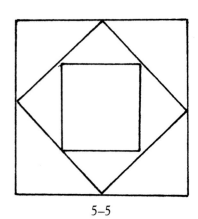

5–5

4. Place a fabric D strip faceup on your sewing machine. Top with a block facedown. Sew, butting in new blocks. See 5–6. Cut as shown in 5–4.

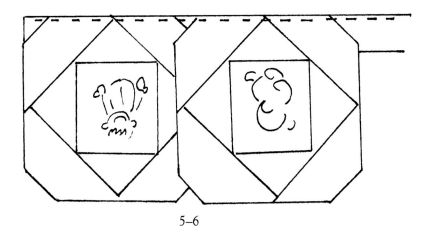

5–6

Continue attaching a fabric D strip to each side of your block. See 5–7 for how the block should look with the fabric D strip on all four sides; then refer to 5–4 for cutting.

5. The fabric E triangles are your corners for the blocks. Sew one in each corner so that your block will look like the one in 5–8. Press.

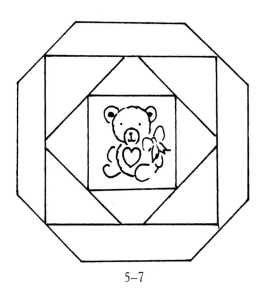

5–7

5–8 Finished Block

6. Your quilt top will have five rows, and each row will contain four blocks.

7. Add borders as directed in the Speed Techniques section, and finish the quilt as you like.

Beggar's Block

6 Beggar's Block

This quilt is so named because of restrictions on cloth making in America by Britain during the mid-1700s. It became a neighborly custom to beg friends for scraps of old dresses or neckties to put into this quilt.

YARDAGE

Fabric A	⅓ yard
Fabric B	3 yards
Fabric C	3¼ yards
Fabric D	¾ yard

CUTTING

Fabric A	two strips 5 × 45 inches
	(cut into 5 × 5 inch squares)
Fabric B	fifteen strips 2 × 45 inches
Fabric B	six strips 3 × 45 inches
Fabric B, first border	eight strips 5 × 45 inches
Fabric C	thirty strips 2 × 45 inches
Fabric C	eight strips 5 × 45 inches
Fabric C, third border	eight strips 5 × 45 inches
Fabric D, second border	eight strips 3 × 45 inches

SEWING DIRECTIONS

Size: 72 × 81 inches

1. Sew your 2-inch strips as shown in 6–1, for a total of fifteen times. Press.
2. Measure down 5 inches and cut (see 6–2). You'll get nine cuts per strip. You'll need a total of 128 to construct sixteen blocks.
3. Construct your block, as shown in 6–3, using fabric A as the center square for a total of sixteen blocks.
4. Sew four blocks together to form a row. Repeat for a total of four times.
   Sew in between each row a 3-inch fabric B strip.
5. Attach your borders as directed in the Speed Techniques section. Finish the quilt as you wish.

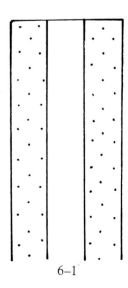

6–1

Beggar's Block

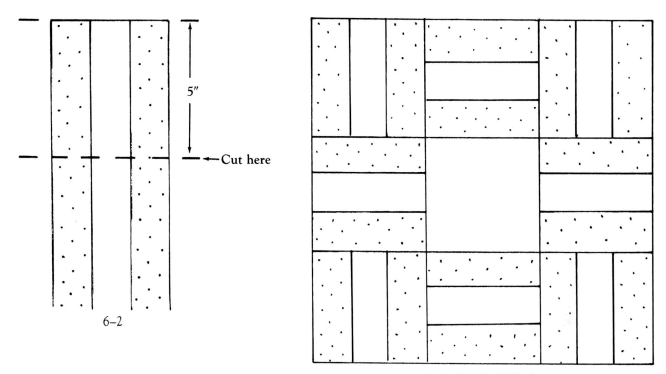

6–2

5″

←Cut here

6–3 Finished Block

43

44   **Four-Block**

7 Four-Block

This is a re-creation of an 1870 quilt made in red and white that was also called Indian Puzzle. This pattern was especially popular in the pioneer days of Indiana. In the mid-1800s, "turkey red" was widely used. So, that's probably when this Four-Block pattern was most popular in America.

YARDAGE

Fabric A	4 yards
Fabric B	3 yards

CUTTING

Fabric A	seven strips 6½ × 45 inches
Fabric A, border	eight strips 3 × 45 inches
Fabric B	seven strips 6½ × 45 inches

The sewing directions include more cutting; so, don't panic because of all the fabric left. You'll use it.

SEWING DIRECTIONS

Size: 72 × 84 inches

1. With right sides together, sew a fabric A and a fabric B 6½-inch strip together lengthwise. Repeat for a total of seven times. See 7–1.

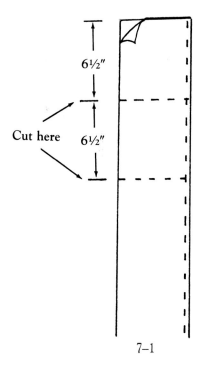

7–1

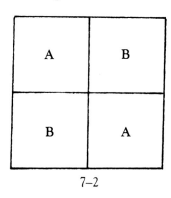

7–2

2. Measure down from the top 6½ inches and cut (see 7–1). Press open. Sew two of your cut pieces together so that your finished block will look like the one in 7–2. Repeat for a total of twenty times.

3. Press and measure your finished blocks. They should be between 12 and 12½ inches square. They may differ in size because of how the seam is sewn.

4. Whatever the size of your blocks, cut ten the same size from fabric A and ten from fabric B. Four of the solid fabric A blocks should be cut on the diagonal to form eight triangles. One more of the fabric A blocks should be cut on the diagonal and then cut on the diagonal in the opposite direction. (See 7–3.) So, you have cut a total of five blocks.

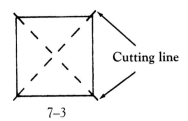

7–3

5. From the ten solid fabric B blocks, cut four on the diagonal to form eight triangles. Cut one more on the diagonal and then on the opposite diagonal. (See 7–3.) Again, you've cut a total of five blocks.

6. Now put your quilt top together, as shown in 7–4.

7. Attach borders as directed in "Adding Borders" in Speed Techniques. Finish the quilt using whatever method you prefer.

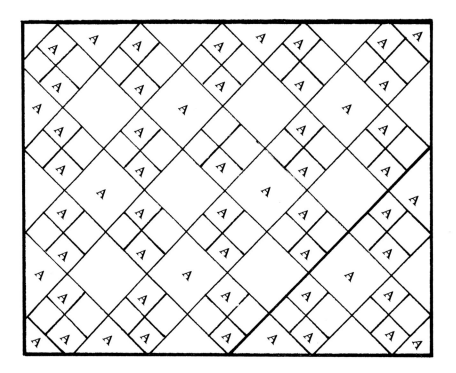

7–4

Four-Block

Victorian Lap Quilt

8 Victorian Lap Quilt

The Victorian Lap Quilt is similar to the "crazy quilts" that first appeared around the 1830s but didn't become popular until the 1880s. Satin, lace, and velvet give this quilt a luxurious feeling.

YARDAGE

Velvet (different colors)	4 yards
Satin (different colors)	4 yards
Different laces	20 yards
Heavy cotton	4 yards
Satin for backing	5 yards

(These yardage measurements are approximate.)

CUTTING

Heavy cotton	twenty squares 12 × 12 inches
Heavy cotton and first border of satin	four strips 4 × 45 inches
Heavy cotton and second border of velvet	four strips 4 × 45 inches

SEWING DIRECTIONS

Size: 52 × 68 inches

Cut your velvets and satins in different widths. Then cut to fit your squares. We will be making ten satin-and-lace squares and ten velvet-and-satin squares.

How to make the satin-and-lace squares:

    1. Finger-press, on the diagonal, one of your 12-inch-by-12-inch squares. Center a piece of satin down the diagonal line. Lay a strip of lace on top of that, top with another piece of satin right side down, and stitch as shown in 8–1.

    2. Open the top piece of satin up so that the right side is now faceup; at this point, you may want to secure your lace with a zigzag or running stitch. Top with lace and satin or just satin. With the right sides together, stitch as shown in 8–2.

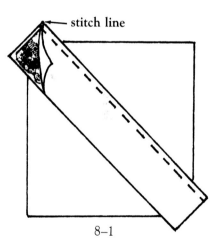

stitch line

8–1

3. Open the top satin up and continue to build this way until one side of your square is completed. Build on the opposite side of the square in the same fashion.

4. When the entire square is covered with satin and lace, turn it over and trim off the satin and lace edges (see 8–3).

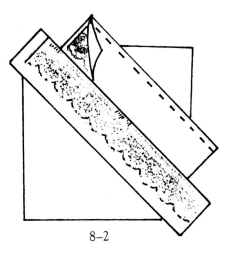

8–2

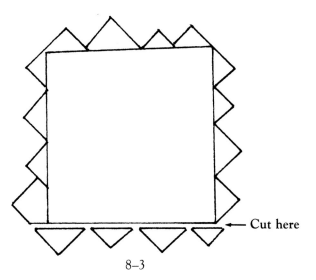

←— **Cut here**

8–3

To make the velvet-and-satin squares:

Sew the same as for the satin-and-lace squares, mixing and matching fabric to fit your taste.

Note: I try to make two or three squares at the same time; this really speeds things along. It's amazing how much time can be spent on trying to come up with different color combinations.

To make the quilt top:

Sew five rows, each row containing four squares. Add borders as directed in Speed Techniques and finish the quilt as you like.

Victorian Lap Quilt

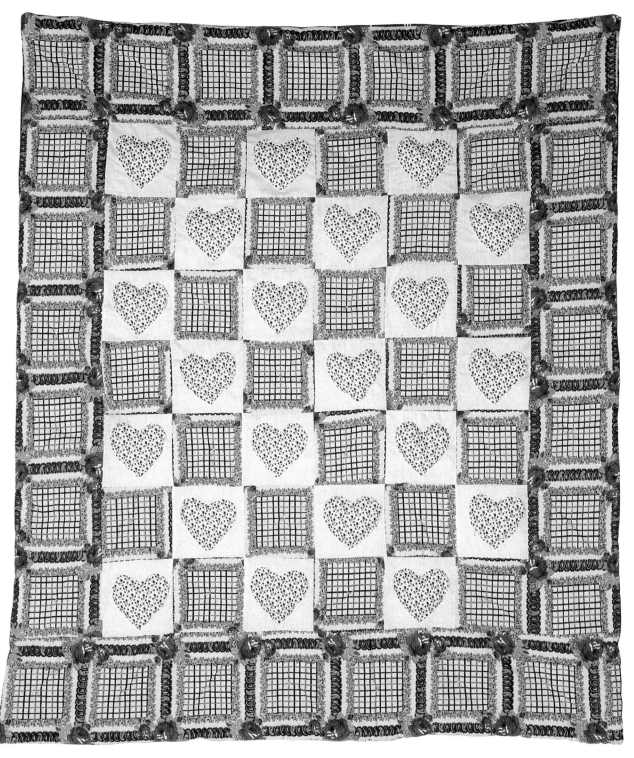

Puffed-Heart Quilt

9 Puffed-Heart Quilt

Hearts have been used in decorations to symbolize love since the mid-1500s. And quilters have been no exception. However, the belief was that hearts only went on wedding quilts or you would never find true love.

YARDAGE

Fabric A	¾ yard
Fabric B	¾ yard
Fusible interfacing	3 yards
Fabric C	¾ yard
First border	¾ yard
Second border	1 yard
Third border	1½ yards

CUTTING

Fabric A and interfacing	twenty-one hearts (use the template provided)
Fabrics B and C	twenty-one squares each 7 × 7 inches
First border	eight strips 3 × 45 inches
Second border	eight strips 4 × 45 inches
Third border	eight strips 5 × 45 inches

SEWING DIRECTIONS

Size: 63 × 63 inches

1. Using the twenty-one hearts from fabric A and the interfacing as well as the twenty-one 7-inch fabric B squares, follow the directions for "Speed appliqué" in the Speed Techniques section. However, before applying the warm iron, but after being reversed, put a little stuffing inside the slit in the back of the heart. This will puff it up. Apply and sew as directed.

2. Now let's sew our blocks. The first, third, fifth, and seventh rows will have the following: heart square, fabric C square, heart, fabric C, heart, and finally fabric C square. The second, fourth, and sixth rows will have the following: fabric C square, heart square, fabric C, heart, fabric C, and, last, heart square.

3. Sew your rows together, add borders (according to the instructions in Speed Techniques), and finish the quilt as you like.

Puffed Heart Template

Puffed-Heart Quilt

Love Apple

10 Love Apple

This pattern dates back to the late 1700s. The tomato was known as the "love apple." Native to the tropics, tomatoes were grown in the United States primarily in flower gardens for their beautiful red fruit. But the fruit was never eaten, until around the early or mid-1800s, since it was believed to be poisonous.

YARDAGE

Fabric A	½ yard
Fabric B	5 yards
Fabric C	3 yards

CUTTING

Fabric A	3 strips 2 × 45 inches
Fabric B	sixty strips 2½ × 45 inches (to save fabric, cut forty-five strips and sew the short ends together, then cut more strips and sew together if needed)
Fabric B	ten strips 1¾ × 45 inches
Fabric B	six strips 1 × 45 inches
Fabric C	twenty-nine strips 2½ × 45 inches (cut four of these strips into sixty 2½ × 2½ inch squares)
Fabric C	four strips 5½ × 45 inches

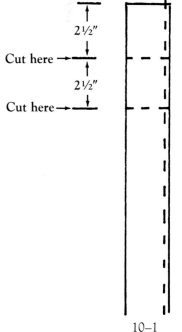

2½"

Cut here →

2½"

Cut here →

10–1

SEWING DIRECTIONS

Size: 85 × 85 inches

This quilt requires sixty squares to complete.

   1. Sew the length of a fabric A strip to a 1¾-inch fabric B strip, with right sides together. Repeat for a total of three times.
   2. Measure down from the top 2 inches and cut. Continue until all the strips just sewn have been cut into 2-inch segments. See 10–1. You will need sixty of these.

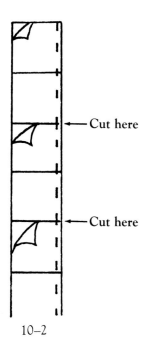

10–2

3. Place a 1¾-inch fabric B strip faceup on your sewing machine. Lay a piece from Step 2 facedown, with the fabric B square to the top. Stitch the length, butting in pieces, until all sixty pieces have been sewn to a 1¾-inch fabric B strip. Cut apart, as shown in 10–2.

4. Lay a 2½-inch fabric C strip faceup on your sewing machine. Top with a piece from Step 3 facedown. Have the last strip added to the top and perpendicular to the strip on your sewing machine. Stitch the length, butting in new blocks, until all sixty pieces have been added to a 2½-inch fabric C strip. Cut apart, as shown in 10–3.

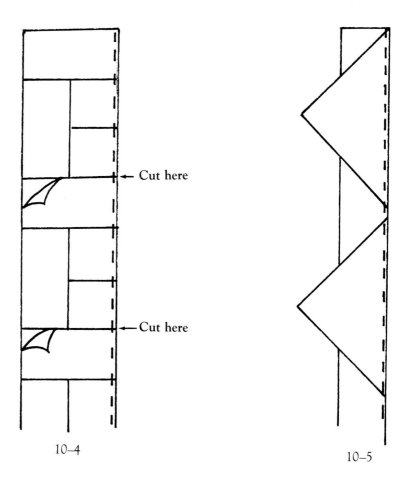

10–4

10–5

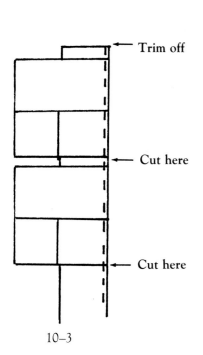

10–3

5. We will now be building on our square from Step 4. Lay a 2½-inch fabric C strip faceup on your sewing machine. Place a sewn square facedown on the strip. (Remember, the last strip added will be to the top and perpendicular to the strip on your sewing machine.) Stitch the length, butting in new squares, until all sixty squares have been added to a 2½-inch fabric C strip. Cut apart, as shown in 10–4. Press and set aside.

6. Cut your sixty 2½-inch squares on the diagonal to form 120 triangles. Place a 1-inch fabric B strip faceup on your sewing machine. Lay one of the triangles facedown, with the longest sides to the right. Sew the length, butting in, until sixty have been added to a 1-inch fabric B strip. See 10–5.

7. Without cutting, add a triangle to the opposite side of your 1-inch strip. See 10–6. Press open. Then cut apart, as shown in 10–7. This is the stem of your love apple.

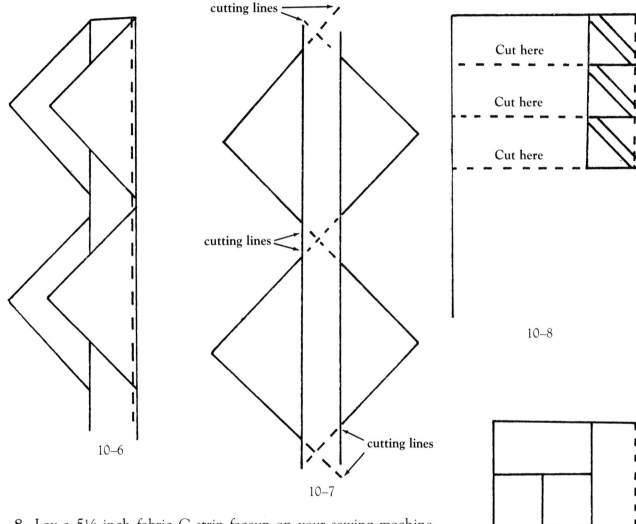

cutting lines

cutting lines

cutting lines

Cut here

Cut here

Cut here

10–6

10–7

10–8

10–9

8. Lay a 5½-inch fabric C strip faceup on your sewing machine. Top with a stem piece facedown. Sew down the length, butting in the stem pieces, until all sixty have been added to a 5½-inch fabric C strip. Cut apart, as shown in 10–8.

9. Set your piece from Step 5 faceup on your sewing machine, with the fabric A block to the upper right.

Lay your piece from Step 8 facedown, with the stem block to the bottom, and sew the length. See 10–9. Repeat for a total of sixty times.

10. Using the techniques shown in Steps 3–5, attach a 2½-inch fabric B strip to all four sides.

11. Sew your squares together, as shown in 10–10. Finish the quilt as you like.

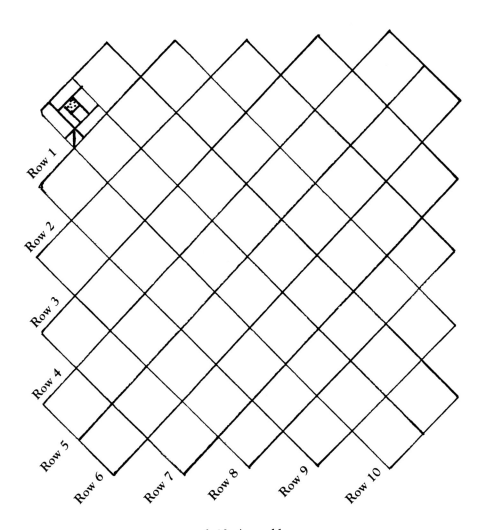

6–10 **Assembly**

Love Apple

Bear's Paw or Hand of Friendship (*see p.* 89)

Wedding Ring or Georgetown Circle (*see p. 25*)

Town Calicos

11 Town Calicos

This Town Calicos quilt design is over 100 years old. Calico, a cotton fabric in which a figured pattern is repeated in 1-inch squares, has been popular since the 1500s.

Many religious quilters felt that only God is perfect, so they would deliberately make a mistake, which they called a "God fear patch" or "square." However, not all errors fall into this category. Let's see how perfectly you can create Town Calicos.

YARDAGE

Fabric A	¾ yard
Fabric B	¾ yard
Fabric C	¾ yard
Fabric D	3¼ yards
Border	1 yard

CUTTING

Fabric A	seven strips 3 × 45 inches
Fabric B	seven strips 3 × 45 inches
Fabric C	seven strips 3 × 45 inches
Fabric D	thirty-six strips 3 × 45 inches
Border	eight strips 4 × 45 inches

SEWING DIRECTIONS

Size: 72 × 85 inches

1. Sew your fabric A, B, and C strips together lengthwise to form sheets, as shown in 11–1. Repeat for a total of seven times. Press flat.

2. Measure down 3 inches and cut, as shown in 11–2. Cut the full length of the sheet. Repeat until all seven sheets are cut into small strips of blocks. You will need at least ninety of these strips of blocks. (You shouldn't come up short since the pattern allows for an extra strip to be cut from each fabric.)

3. Place a fabric D strip faceup on your sewing machine. Lay a strip of blocks facedown, with the fabric A block to the top. Sew down the length of the strip of blocks. Butt in, until all strips of blocks have been attached to a fabric D strip. Cut apart, as shown in 11–3.

11–1

4. Now we will be sewing a fabric D strip on the opposite sides of our strip of blocks. Attach it the same way we attached the fabric D strip on the other side. Do all ninety pieces. We've completed our blocks.

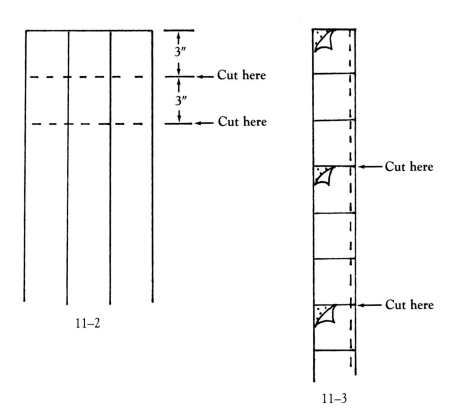

11–2

11–3

5. Sew ten rows, each row containing nine blocks. Use the photo as a guide.

Town Calicos

Queen Charlotte's Crown or Indian Meadow

12 Queen Charlotte's Crown

This quilt dates before the 1770s. This pattern came from Virginia to honor the wife of King George the Third. Queen Charlotte was the last queen America ever had. After the American Revolution, this quilt was renamed "Indian Meadow."

YARDAGE

Fabric A	¾ yard
Fabric B	1¾ yards
Fabric C	½ yard
Fabric D	⅔ yard
Fabric E	⅓ yard
First border	¾ yard
Second border	1 yard
Third border	1½ yards

CUTTING

Fabric A	five strips 5 × 45 inches
Fabric B	five strips 5 × 45 inches
Fabric B	four strips 2½ × 45 inches
Fabric D	two strips 2½ × 45 inches
First border	eight strips 3 × 45 inches
Second border	eight strips 4 × 45 inches
Third border	eight strips 5 × 45 inches

SEWING DIRECTIONS

Size: 60 × 70 inches

1. Following the directions in the Speed Techniques section for "Double Half-Square Triangles," make eighty from the five 5-by-45-inch fabric A strips and the five 5-by-45-inch Fabric B strips. (Make them with the fabric B as the center triangles.) Press open and set aside.

2. With 16½-by-35 inches of both fabric B and C, follow the directions given for "Half-Square Triangles" in Speed Techniques. Use a 5-by-5-inch grid. (This will be seven rows across and three rows

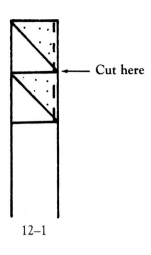

12–1

down.) Sew and cut as directed; then press. You will need forty half-square triangles. Set aside.

3. With 11-by-25 inches of both fabrics D and E, follow the directions for "Half-Square Triangles." Make 5-by-5-inch squares on your grid. (This will be five rows across and two rows down.) Sew and cut as directed, press, and set aside. You'll need twenty.

4. Using 6-by-30-inches of fabrics D and E, make a grid of 3-inch squares. (This will be ten rows across and two rows down.) Follow the directions for "Half-Square Triangles." Sew and cut as directed. Press and divide into two piles, each containing twenty.

5. Place a 2½-inch fabric D strip faceup on your sewing machine. Lay facedown a piece from one of your piles in Step 4, with fabric D in the upper-right-hand corner. (See 12–1.) Sew the length, butting in new pieces, until all twenty have been added to a fabric D strip. Cut apart, as shown in 12–1.

6. Still working with the pieces from Step 5, sew one to a piece from Step 1 so that the finished piece will look like the one shown in 12–2.

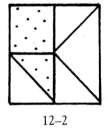

12–2

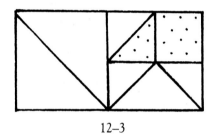

12–3

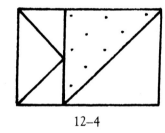

12–4

7. Now sew a piece from Step 6 to the pieces from Step 2. The finished item should look like the one in 12–3. Repeat for a total of twenty times; then set aside.

8. Sew a piece from Step 1 to a piece from Step 3 so that it will look like 12–4. Repeat for a total of twenty times.

9. Place a 2½-inch fabric B strip faceup on your sewing machine. Top with a piece from Step 1. Stitch the length, butting in new pieces, until twenty have been added to a fabric B strip, as shown in 12–5, and twenty have been added to a fabric B strip, as shown in 12–6. Cut apart as directed in the illustration.

10. Attach a piece from Step 8 to a piece from Step 9 (12–5) so that it will look like 12–7. Repeat for a total of twenty times. Set aside until Step 12.

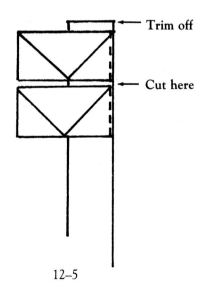

12–5

11. Sew a piece from Step 2 to a piece from Step 4 so that it will look like 12–8. Repeat for a total of twenty times.

12. Sew a piece from Step 10 to one from Step 11 so that it will look like 12–9. Repeat for a total of twenty times.

13. Sew the piece from Step 12 to the piece from Step 7 so that, when finished, it will look like 12–10. Repeat for a total of twenty times.

14. The piece from Step 9 (12–6) fits into the lower-right-hand corner of your block. Sew in place. Your finished block should look like the one shown in 12–11.

15. Add borders, following the instructions in Speed Techniques, and finish the quilt as you like.

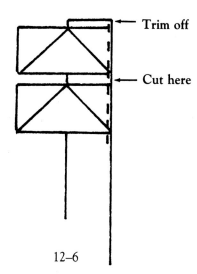

12–6

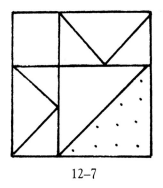

12–7

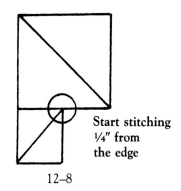

Start stitching ¼" from the edge

12–8

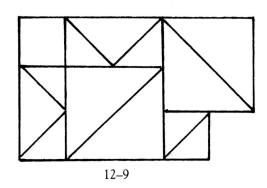

12–9

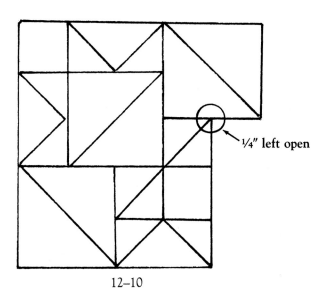

¼" left open

12–10

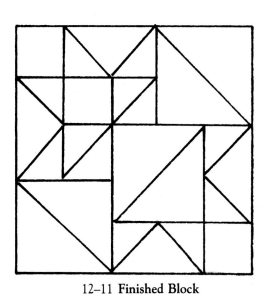

12–11 **Finished Block**

Queen Charlotte's Crown or Indian Meadow (*see* p. 69)

Framed Quilt (*see p. 11*)

Brick House (*see p. 77*)

Butterfly Quilt (*see p. 33*)

Brick House

13   Brick House

This pattern dates to the mid-1700s, as far as I could find. Little is known about its history, but it is one of my favorites.

YARDAGE

Fabric A	¼ yard
Fabric B	¾ yard
Fabric C	¾ yard
Fabric D	2 yards
First border	¾ yard
Second border	1 yard
Third border	1½ yards

CUTTING

Fabric A	two strips 2½ × 45 inches (this is your center square; now cut your strips into thirty 2½- × -2½-inch squares)
Fabric B	eight strips 2½ × 45 inches
Fabric C	eight strips 2½ × 45 inches
Fabric D	fourteen strips 4½ × 45 inches
First border	eight strips 3 × 45 inches
Second border	eight strips 4 × 45 inches
Third border	eight strips 5 × 45 inches

SEWING DIRECTIONS

Size: 70 × 78 inches

1. Sew the length of a fabric B strip to a fabric C strip, with right sides together. Repeat for a total of eight times. Press open.

2. Measure down from the top 2½ inches and cut, until all the strip has been cut into segments of 2½ by 4½ inches. Cut the remaining seven strips this way (see 13–1).

3. Place a fabric D strip faceup on your sewing machine. Lay one of your newly cut pieces facedown, with the fabric A block to the top. Stitch the length and butt in another piece. Continue until 120 pieces have been added to a fabric D strip. Cut as shown in 13–2. (This is called a *triple block.*)

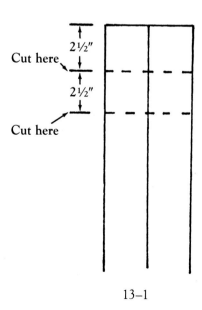

13–1

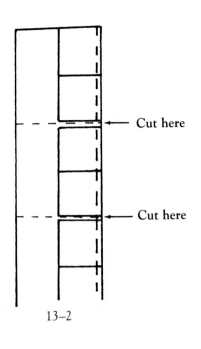

13–2

Cut here

Cut here

4. Attach a fabric A square in the lower-right-hand corner of one triple block. See 13–3. Repeat for a total of thirty times.

5. Next, sew another triple block onto your pieces from the last step. It should look like 13–4.

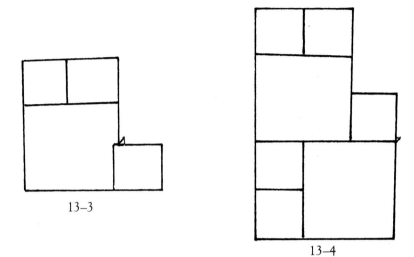

13–3

13–4

6. Attach another triple block to your pieces from the last step. It should look like 13–5.

7. Remove ½ inch of stitching in the upper-right-hand corner of the center square, as shown in 13–6.

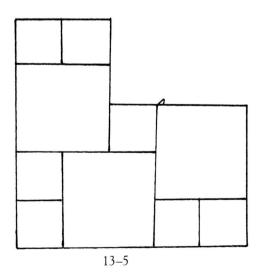

13–5

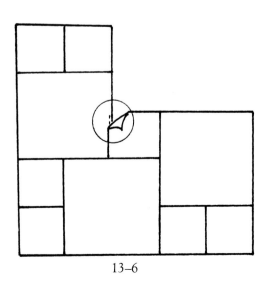

13–6

78

8. Lay your piece from the last step faceup, as shown in 13–7. Top with a triple block facedown, and sew as shown in 13–8.

9. Join your last remaining opening so that your finished block will look like the one in 13–9.

10. Sew six rows, with each row containing five blocks.

11. Refer to "Adding Borders" in the Speed Techniques section. Then attach borders and finish the quilt as you like.

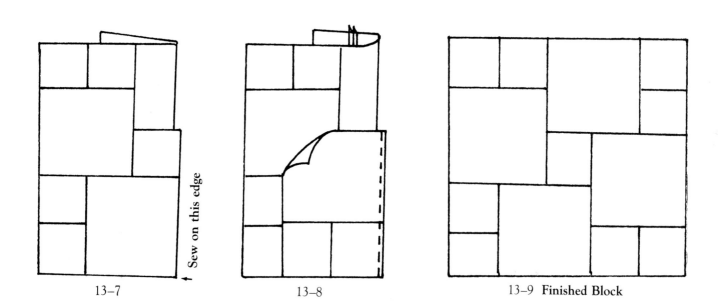

13–7   13–8   13–9 **Finished Block**

Signature Quilt

14 Signature Quilt

Signature quilts, or album quilts, were used as a way to keep records of family and friends. This pattern is a re-creation of one thought to have been made around the 1870s.

YARDAGE

Fabric A	1¼ yards
Fabric B	1¼ yards
First border	¾ yard
Second border	1½ yards
Third border	1¾ yards

CUTTING

Fabrics A and B	twelve squares 12 × 12 inches
First border	eight strips 3 × 45 inches
Second border	eight strips 5 × 45 inches
Third border	eight strips 6 × 45 inches

SEWING DIRECTIONS

Size: 64 × 88 inches

1. Cut your 12-inch squares on the diagonal to form forty-eight triangles.

2. Sew a fabric A triangle to a fabric B triangle, on the diagonal, a total of twenty-four times. After pressing, cut again on the diagonal in the opposite direction of the last cut. (See 14–1.)

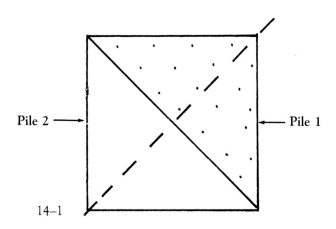

Pile 2 ⟶   ⟵ Pile 1

14–1

3. Working with Pile 1, sew two together on the diagonal. Repeat for a total of twelve times. Do the same with Pile 2. (See 14–1.)

4. Now you have twenty-four blocks that look like 14–2. Sew six rows, with each row containing four blocks.

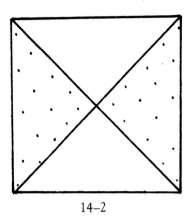

14–2

5. Add borders, following the instructions in the Speed Techniques section, and finish the quilt as you like.

9. You have just completed four rows for your quilt top. Sew the short ends of six 2½-by-45-inch fabric B strips. This will make three long strips. These are your joiner strips. Use them to join the rows together.

10. Attach borders as directed in Speed Techniques. Finish the quilt as you like.

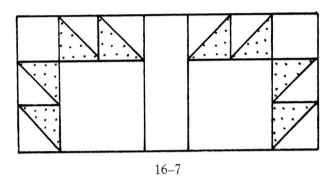

16–7

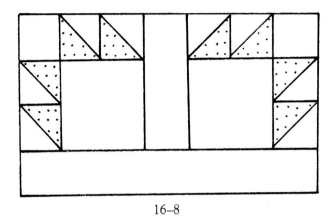

16–8

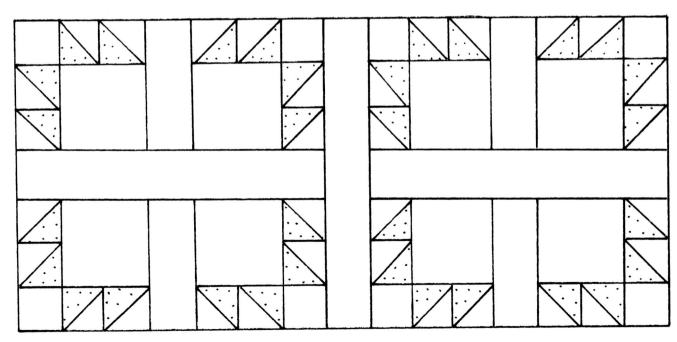

16–9 **Finished Blocks**

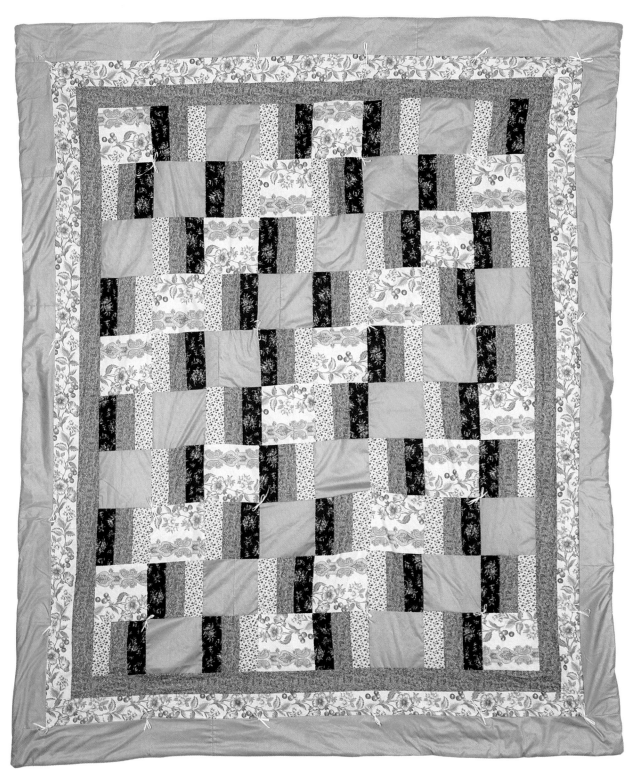

Bright Hopes

17 Bright Hopes

This pattern comes from an old Amish legacy, or sampler, quilt. The sampler quilt was originally called a legacy quilt because it was the means by which a quilter would hand down her best patterns to the next generation of quilters. Why not make your own legacy quilt?

YARDAGE

Fabric A	1 yard
Fabric B	¾ yard
Fabrics C and D	1 yard
Fabric E	1¼ yards
First border	¾ yard
Second border	1 yard
Third border	1½ yards

CUTTING

Fabric A	eight strips 4 × 45 inches
Fabric B	eight strips 2½ × 45 inches
Fabric C	twelve strips 2½ × 45 inches
Fabric D	twelve strips 2½ × 45 inches
Fabric E	sixteen strips 2½ × 45 inches
First border	eight strips 3 × 45 inches
Second border	eight strips 4 × 45 inches
Third border	eight strips 5 × 45 inches

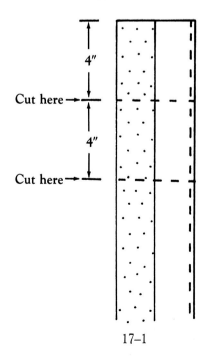

17–1

SEWING DIRECTIONS

Size: 77 × 90 inches

1. Sew lengthwise a 4-inch fabric A strip to a fabric B strip, with right sides together. Repeat for a total of eight times.

Measure down 4 inches and cut. Continue until all eight strips are cut into 4-inch segments. (See 17–1.) You'll need eighty pieces.

2. Lay a fabric C strip faceup on your sewing machine. Top with your squares facedown, having the fabric B strip at the top. Stitch lengthwise, butting in new squares, until all eighty have been added to the fabric C strip. Cut apart, as shown in 17–2.

3. Follow the directions given in step 2; then apply fabric D strips as well as fabric E strips so that your finished block will look like the one in 17–3.

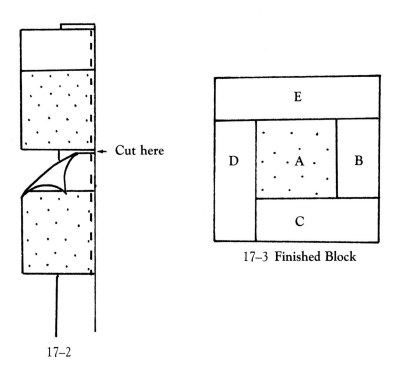

17–2

17–3 Finished Block

4. Sew your quilt top. There should be ten rows, with each row containing eight blocks. Arrange them in an attractive way.

5. Read "Adding Borders" in the Speed Techniques section. Attach borders and finish the quilt as you like.

Bright Hopes

Short-Sided Star

18 Short-Sided Star

Star patterns have been used in quilts since the early 1700s, as far as we know. This modern design, which was arrived at with the cooperation of Jan Lawson, uses a blend of pieced work and appliqué to achieve a pleasing balance of space and solids.

YARDAGE

Fabric A	½ yard
Fabric B	1 yard
Fabric C	1½ yards
Fabric D	1 yard
Fusible interfacing	6 yards
Fabric E, background fabric	5 yards
First border	1 yard
Second border	1½ yards

CUTTING

Fabric A	eight strips 1¾ × 45 inches
Fabric B	sixteen strips 1¾ × 45 inches
Fabric C	twenty-four strips 1¾ × 45 inches
Fabric D	sixteen strips 1¾ × 45 inches
First border	eight strips 2½ × 45 inches
Second border	eight strips 2½ × 45 inches

SEWING DIRECTIONS

Size: 72 × 104 inches

1. Before sewing your strips, review Speed Techniques, beginning on page 13. Then refer to 18–1 and 18–2 to determine the placement of your strips. The illustrations show the 2½ inches that you should leave from the end of each preceding strip when adding another. Sew them one at a time into sets of four until you have eight sets of each group. Press.

2. Cut new strips, at a 45-degree angle, from the sets that you have just sewn. Each strip should measure 2½ inches wide, and you should be able to get ten strips from each fabric block. (This is a generous pattern with leftovers that I often use for a pieced second border, or a nice block in a sampler quilt.) See 18–3.

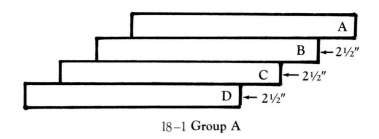

18–1 **Group A**

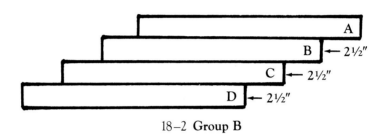

18–2 **Group B**

3. Now we will join the newly created strips together to form one star point. Sew one piece from Group A to one piece from Group B. Repeat for a total of sixty-four times. Press flat. See 18–4.

4. Now go back to Speed Techniques and read "Speed Appliqué" once more. Then, using the star point as your template, cut thirty-two fusible interfacings. (Make sure that the glue side is facedown on the top side of the star point.) Sew and turn as directed in "Speed Appliqué."

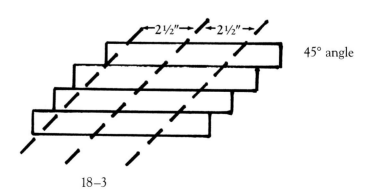

18–3

Short-Sided Star

5. Cut fabric E into two equal parts. Sew the two pieces together, along the selvage edge, to form one piece again.

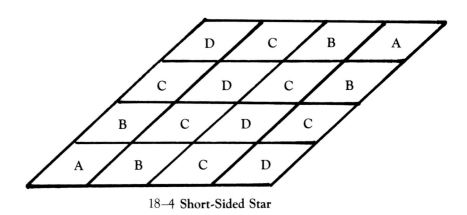

18–4 **Short-Sided Star**

6. Place your star points in position, as shown in 18–5. Press in place; stitch around, as directed in "Speed Appliqué."

7. Read "Adding Borders" in Speed Techniques again. Add borders and finish the quilt as you like.

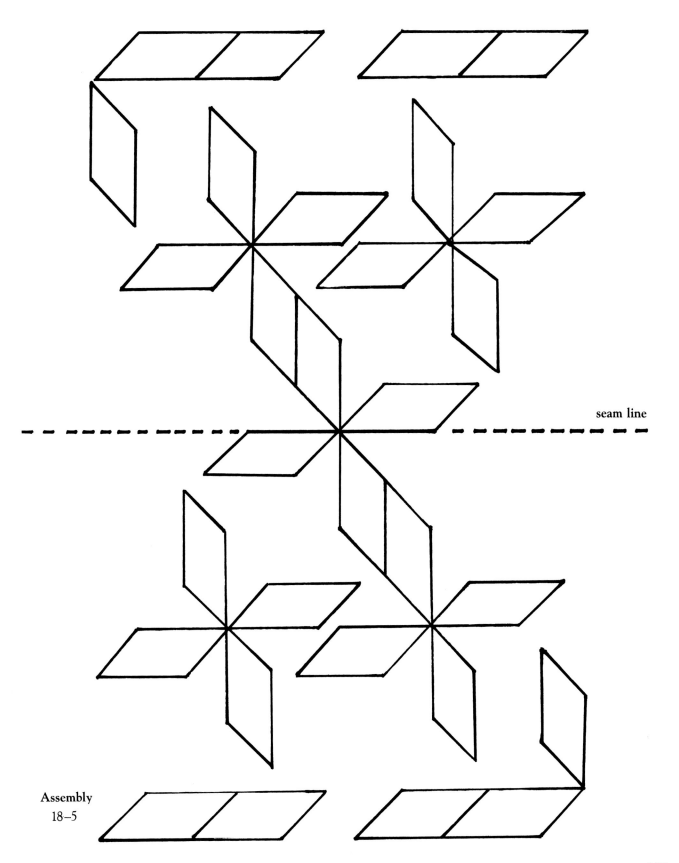

seam line

Assembly
18–5

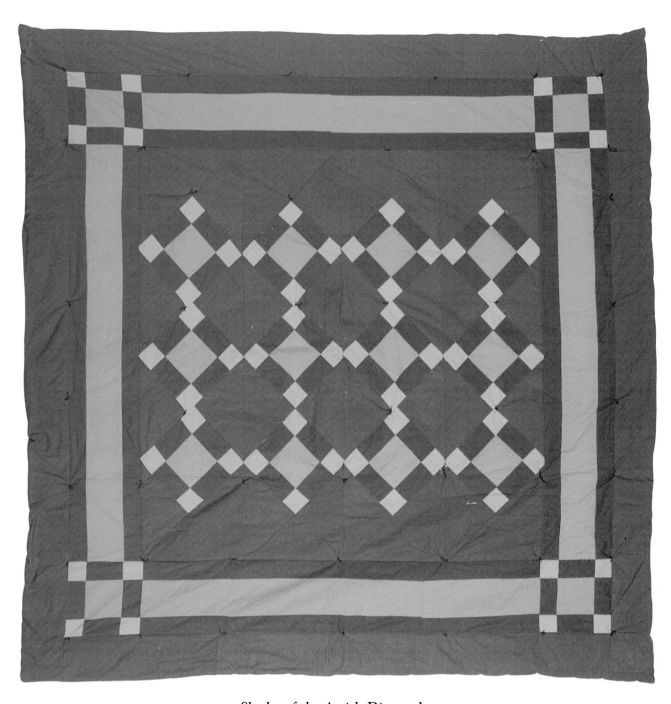

Shades of the Amish Diamond

19 Shades of the Amish Diamond

For over 200 years, quilting has played a very important role in the lives of Amish women. Quilts have allowed women to socialize and to be creative in a way that other household duties do not allow.

YARDAGE

Fabric A (green)	½ yard
Fabric B (purple)	1½ yards
Fabric C (turquoise)	1½ yards
Fabric D (navy blue)	3¾ yards

CUTTING

Fabric A	four strips 2½ × 45 inches
Fabric B	four strips 2½ × 45 inches
Fabric B	two strips 4½ × 45 inches
Fabric C	two strips 4½ × 45 inches
Fabric D	six strips 9 × 45 inches
Fabric D	four strips 12 × 12 squares
Fabric B, first and third border	ten strips 2½ × 45 inches
Fabric C, second border	eight strips 4½ × 45 inches
Fabric D, fourth border	eight strips 6 × 45 inches

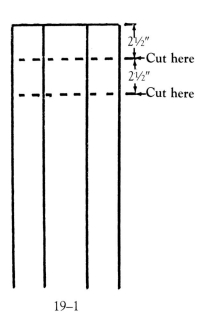

19–1

SEWING DIRECTIONS

Size: 72 × 72 inches

1. Sew two 2½-by-45-inch fabric A green strips lengthwise to a 4½-by-45-inch fabric B strip sandwiched in the middle (see 19–1). Repeat a second time. Measure down 2½ inches and cut, as shown in 19–1. You'll need thirty-two cut pieces. Press open and set aside.

2. Sew, two 2½-by-45-inch fabric B strips lengthwise with one 4½-by-45-inch fabric C strip sandwiched in the middle. (See 19–2). Repeat a second time. Measure down 4½ inches and cut as shown in 19–2. You'll need sixteen cut pieces. Press open.

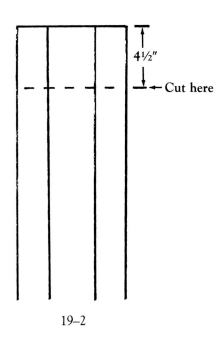

19–2

4½"

← Cut here

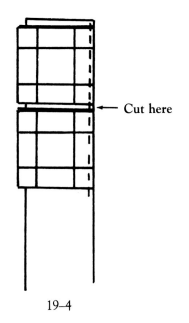

19–4

← Cut here

3. Sew the pieces from steps 1 and 2 to form the square shown in 19–3. Repeat sixteen times in all. Press and set four aside.

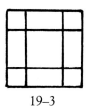

19–3

4. Place a 9-by-45-inch fabric D strip faceup on your sewing machine. Lay your newly sewn square facedown, and sew the length. Butt in new squares until all sixteen squares have been added to a fabric D strip. Check 19–4 to see how to cut them apart. Then sew them together to form a row of three patched blocks and three solid blocks. Attach another solid block on the end so that you have a row of four solid and three patched blocks alternated. Now refer to 19–5 to see how to cut your rows.

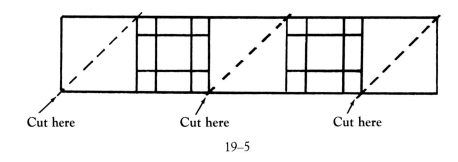

Cut here   Cut here   Cut here

19–5

5. Take the four 12-inch squares, and cut them on the diagonal to form eight triangles. Now study 19–6 to see how to sew everything together.

6. Pair off and sew the short ends of your borders as directed in Speed Techniques. However, you will attach the borders differently because of the square in the corner. Sew your first border to the sides only, then sew the second border to the sides only, and finally, sew the third border to the sides only. Press and measure across the top, but do not include the borders in the measurement. Add ½ inch. This is the measurement for the top and bottom borders. Sew the borders together just as you did for the sides only, but do not attach them to the quilt top yet. Take the four blocks that you set aside in step 3, and sew one to

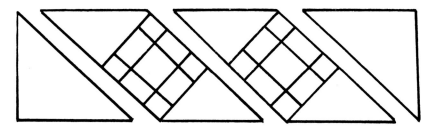

19–6 **Assembly**

each end of the borders. Sew the borders to the top and bottom. Now you can attach the fourth and final border as directed in Speed Techniques. Finish as you like.

Snowball

20 Snowball

The Snowball quilt is a good example of the use of the nine-block pattern. The nine-block has been widely used in the United States since the early 1900s.

YARDAGE

Fabric A (for the snowball)	2¼ yards
Fabric B	1¼ yards
Total of different colors	2½ yards
First border	¾ yard
Second border	1 yard
Third border	1½ yards

CUTTING

Fabric A	six strips 8 × 45 inches (cut strips into forty-two 8 × 8 inch blocks)
Fabric B	twelve strips 3 × 45 inches (cut strips into one-hundred-sixty-eight 3 × 3 inch blocks)
Strips of different colors	twenty-seven strips 3 × 45 inches
First border	eight strips 3 × 45 inches
Second border	eight strips 4½ × 45 inches
Third border	eight strips 6 × 45 inches

SEWING DIRECTIONS

Size: 85 × 100 inches

1. Sew and cut fabric A and B squares as shown in 20–1. Press and set aside.
2. Working with the twenty-seven multi-colored strips, sew them lengthwise in sets of three. Continue until you have nine sets of three. Press.

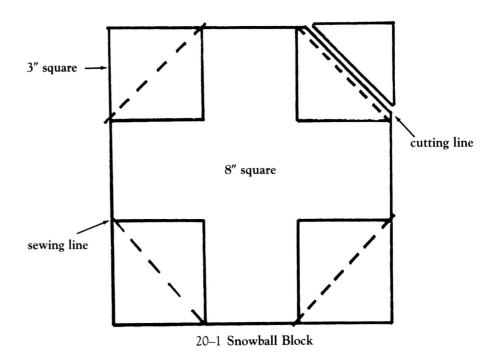

3" square →

cutting line

8" square

sewing line

20-1 Snowball Block

3. Measure 3 inches down from the top and cut. See 20–2. Continue until you finish all nine sets of strips. You'll need one hundred twenty-six strips of squares to make the forty-two blocks needed for this pattern.

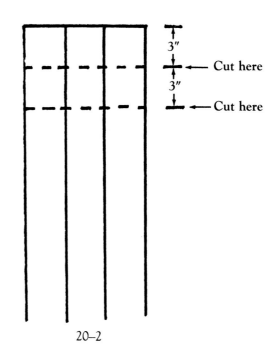

3"

← Cut here

3"

← Cut here

20–2

4. Sew your strip of squares together to form a nine-block. See 20–3. Repeat until you have forty-two blocks done. Press.

20–3 **Nine-Block**

5. Now we're ready to assemble our quilt top. Sew eight squares together, alternating one snowball square with one nine-block. Repeat ten times. When you're done, you should have four blocks left over; these can be used for a throw pillow or a block in a sampler quilt.

6. Attach the borders as directed in Speed Techniques. Finish the quilt any way you like.

Stacked Patience Corners

21 Stacked Patience Corners

The common method of creating a quilt one block at a time was developed in the United States. This type of quilt was not widely used in other parts of the world. However, in Ireland, it has been used in a limited way, primarily in the center of the quilt. Then these blocks are called panes.

YARDAGE

Center piece	16½ × 16½ square
Fabric A	1 yard
Fabric B	1½ yards
Fabric C	2½ yards
Fabric D	1 yard
Fabric E	1½ yards
Fabric F	2½ yards
First border	1 yard

CUTTING

Fabric A	nine strips 2½ × 45 inches
Fabric B	fourteen strips 2½ × 45 inches
Fabric C	twelve strips 4½ × 45 inches
Fabric D	nine strips 2½ × 45 inches
Fabric E	fourteen strips 2½ × 45 inches
Fabric F	twelve strips 4½ × 45 inches
First border	eight strips 4 × 45 inches

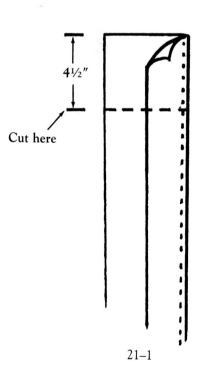

4½"

Cut here

21–1

SEWING DIRECTIONS

Size: 85 × 85 inches

1. Make twenty-four of each block. Let's start with block A. Place a 4½-inch fabric C strip faceup on your sewing machine, and lay facedown a 2½-inch fabric B strip. Sew lengthwise. Repeat for a total of three times. Cut as shown in 21–1. You'll need twenty-four cut pieces in all.

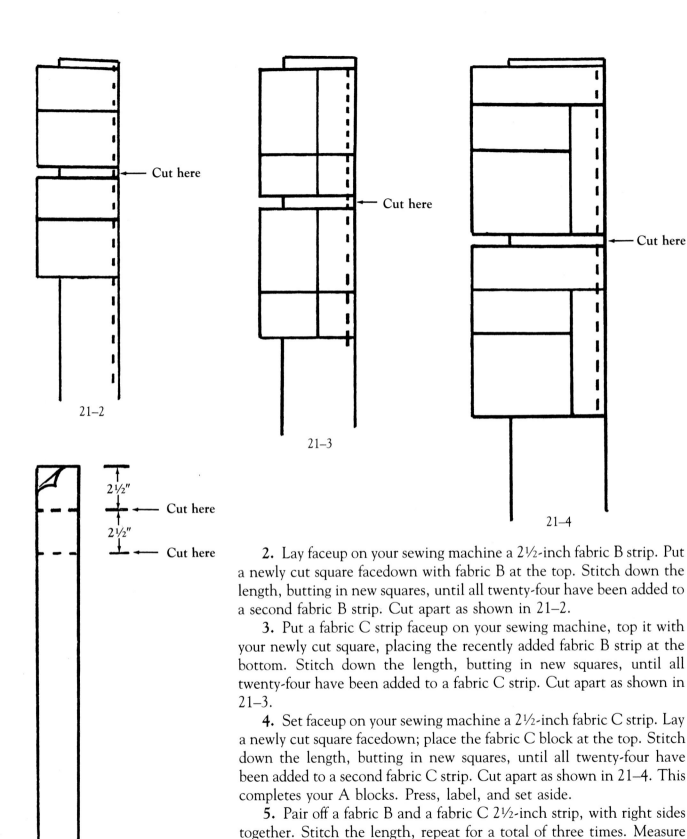

21–2

21–3

21–4

21–5

2. Lay faceup on your sewing machine a 2½-inch fabric B strip. Put a newly cut square facedown with fabric B at the top. Stitch down the length, butting in new squares, until all twenty-four have been added to a second fabric B strip. Cut apart as shown in 21–2.

3. Put a fabric C strip faceup on your sewing machine, top it with your newly cut square, placing the recently added fabric B strip at the bottom. Stitch down the length, butting in new squares, until all twenty-four have been added to a fabric C strip. Cut apart as shown in 21–3.

4. Set faceup on your sewing machine a 2½-inch fabric C strip. Lay a newly cut square facedown; place the fabric C block at the top. Stitch down the length, butting in new squares, until all twenty-four have been added to a second fabric C strip. Cut apart as shown in 21–4. This completes your A blocks. Press, label, and set aside.

5. Pair off a fabric B and a fabric C 2½-inch strip, with right sides together. Stitch the length, repeat for a total of three times. Measure down 2½ inches, and cut. Continue until you have twenty-four pieces. See 21–5.

Cut here

Cut here

Cut here

2½"

Cut here

2½"

Cut here

112

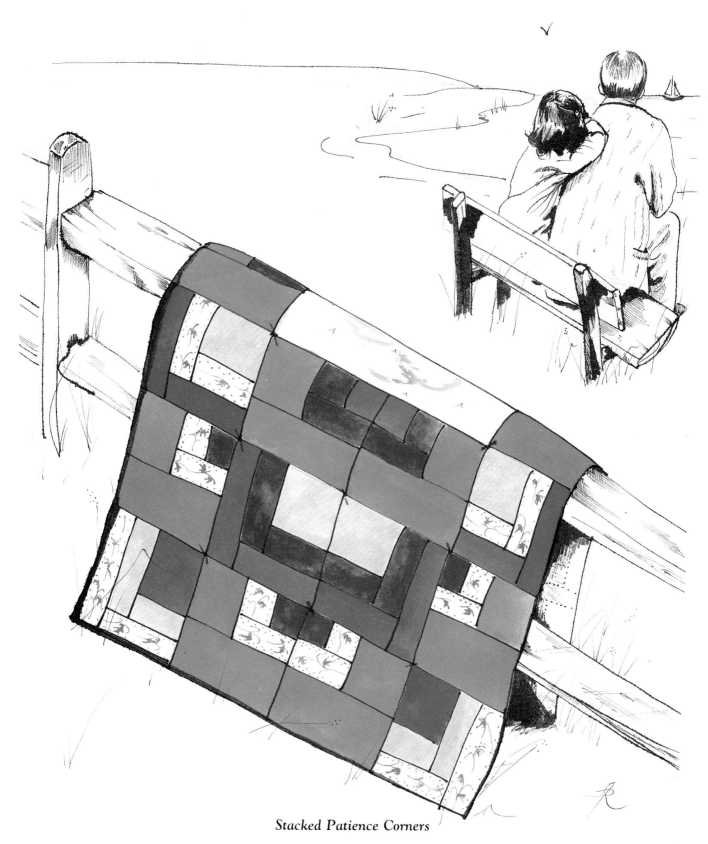

Stacked Patience Corners

6. Lay a fabric C strip faceup on your sewing machine. Place the newly cut squares over it, with the fabric C strip at the top. Stitch down the length, butting in new squares, until you've added a second fabric C strip to all twenty-four. Cut apart as shown in 21–6.

7. Place a 4½-inch fabric A strip faceup on your sewing machine. Lay your newly sewn square facedown with the fabric B strip at the upper left. Stitch down the length, butting in new squares, until all twenty-four have been added to a fabric A strip. See 21–7.

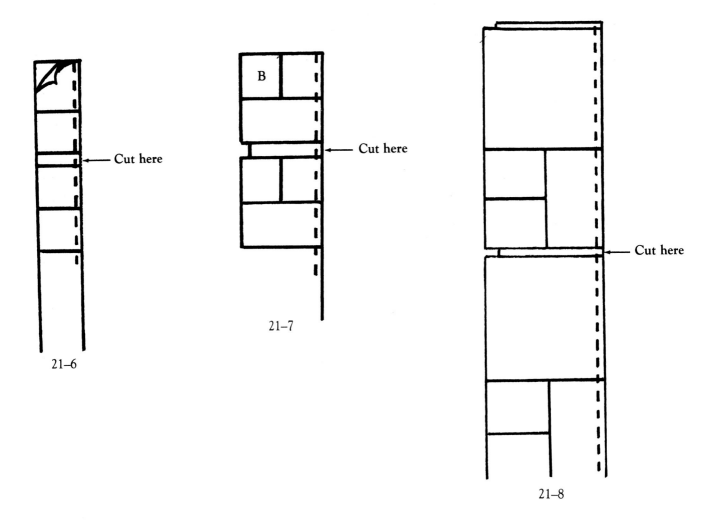

21–6

21–7

21–8

8. Set a 4½-inch fabric A strip faceup on your sewing machine. Place your newly sewn square facedown with the fabric A strip at the top. Stitch down the length, butting in new squares, until all twenty-four have been added to your fabric A strip. See 21–8. This completes your C blocks. Press, label, and set aside.

9. To make your B blocks, repeat the steps used to create block C, using fabrics D, E, and F. You will need twenty-four blocks of these as well.

D	C	B	A	D	D	A	B	C	D
C	B	A	D	C	C	D	A	B	C
B	A	D	C	B	B	C	D	A	B
A	D	C	B	A	A	B	C	D	A
D	C	B	A			A	B	C	D
D									D
	D						D		
		D				D			
			D		D				
D				D	D				D

21–9 **Assembly**

Point the blocks towards the middle of the quilt top.

10. To make your D blocks, repeat the steps used to create block A, using fabrics F, E, and D. You will need twenty-four of these blocks.

11. Sew your blocks together as shown in 21–9. Add borders if you wish.

Shades of the Amish Diamond (*see* p. 103)

Snowball (see p. 107)

Quilting Time Line

A Quick Look at the History of Quilting

Quilt, from the old French word *cuilte*, which was later replaced by the Latin word *culoitra*, meaning "stuffed mattress, or cushion."

3400 B.C.E.	In Egypt, archaeologists have found a statue dating back to 3400 B.C.E. of a pharaoh wearing a quilted garment.
980 B.C.E.	The most ancient pieced, appliquéd work known to date is in the Cairo Museum. A few of the colors in it are pink, purple, and green.
1st century	Jewish historian Flavius Josephus tells of the beautiful quilted tapestry that hung in the temple Herod built. In Mongolia, a quilted floor covering was found dated at this time period.
4th century	One of the oldest wooden blocks for printing on fabric was found in Egypt, dating to the fourth century. The blocks were used to print a design on a child's garment. Little advancement was made in fabric print until the 1740s. A vegetable dye was used for the design. The most frequently used colors were pink, indigo, all shades of red, brownish green, yellow, and purple. More than one color could be printed at a time.
From 600	Pieced work was used for banners and flags as well as in the home.
1000–1300	During the Crusades, the Arabs wore quilted clothing, both for protection and comfort.
1200s	The French poem "*La Lai del Desire*" from this time period describes a checkerboard-pattern quilt made of two different silk cloths.
From 1500s	Most early quilts were finished with a heavy brand

1500s *cont.*	of linen, calico, or silk placed over a hemmed lining and patchwork. Sometimes piping cord was used, which preserved the edges and was easy to replace. Unbleached calico was used as a background for colored-pattern fabrics. Today, a fabric is called calico when a pattern is repeated in 1-inch squares. Originally, calico was heavier than today's muslin fabric, and was imported from India. It was fashionable in Europe for the well-to-do to wear quilted and pieced clothing.
1620s	Most materials for American quilts were imported.
1692	Earliest reference to quilts being listed in wills with household items.
1700s	Florence Peto speaks of an appliquéd coverlet, brought to America from England by a young bride, that was finished by a second worker by tying it with blue and white cotton thread.
1708	The first known time that quilting joined forces with pieced work: "Leven's Hall" quilt.
1740–1750	The technique of printing on fabric with copper plates engraved with a pattern comes into use. This allowed for a finer and more detailed pattern, but only one color could be printed at a time. To keep printing costs down, bold lines were printed, then "pencilling" was done by young girls.
1750	In Scotland, homespun woolens were made into pieced work.
1750s	No cotton piece works were found before this time; they were all linen, silk, velvets, and calico. During the 1750s, the imported cottons from France and India along with American-grown cotton started to gain acceptance. (Cotton became a staple American crop.)
1771	Date of the first-known "Feather Star" quilt.
1775–1800	Dates of some of the oldest surviving American-made quilts.

1780	Date of the earliest strip-patterned piece work, by non-native Americans; it was a coverlet.
1780s	Quilting became a part of girls' training both in the home and at school, for those who could go. Many quilts made by children began to show up by the early 1800s.
1790s	Unpadded day quilts and top covers for beds became popular, and stayed popular for almost thirty-five years.
1795–1805	During this period, centers of quilts were usually large appliquéd birds, trees, and flowers, with pieced work sewn around them.
Early 1800s	All-over quilts make a showing. Examples: "Trip Around the World" and "Tumbling Block."
1800	In the United States, especially on the East Coast, a real love for quilting as a pastime had developed. People had more leisure time and quilting bees provided them with an opportunity to enjoy one another's company; so, more fancy quilts were made as a result. Cottons became cheap, including printed cottons.
1807	"Drab" colors had almost disappeared from prints. But as long as fabric pieces remained, they continued to show up in patchwork.
1810s	Elizabeth Fry of England taught imprisoned women to do patchwork and pieced work, and if they were transported overseas she saw to it that they had enough material for the long trip. Then they could sell their work upon arrival and start to make a living at quilting.
1815	Common use of mechanical rollers for faster printing on fabric.
1800–1850	Finishing quilts with fringes became popular. This was also the time "fan quilts" began to appear.

1830s	As with clothes, the fashion of quilts changed. Now a new style of quilts came into being, "crazy quilts." Instead of cottons and calicos, they were made of velvets, satins, and rich brocade. There was a real acceptance of all-over quilts. Muslin began to appear.
1840s	Diaries from this period have been found that contain entries of how girls couldn't go out to play until they had cut out their daily number of required pieces that would be sewn together that evening or sometime soon. Evidence that fathers and sons would help cut out templates and even do some sewing on the quilts is also found in diaries and letters.
1840–1890	Framed quilts make a showing; they are quilts that contain a series of borders or frames within the body of the quilt.
1840–1940	The "traditional" period for Amish quilts, which featured sharp color contrasts and always solid fabric.
1850	"Turkey red" is the most popular color in quilts. This was the first time binding was cut on the bias and sewn on mitred corners.
1850–1900	Pleated or ruffled edging become popular ways to finish a quilt.
1856	A painting by T. W. Wood documents the fact that quilting was not done only by women. It depicts a Private T. Walker piecing a quilt top, and, from the looks of it, he's doing a great job.
1861–1865	"U.S. Civil War quilts" were sold for bandages and other medical uses.
Late 1800s	Popular colors in quilts are purple, mauve, blue, pink, and buff yellow.
1879	The Smithsonian Institution has a beautiful machine-sewn quilt in its collection.

1880	"Crazy quilts" become popular.
1890s	A farm journal dated in the late 1890s said, "Quilts have had their day."
1910–1920s	The lost generation of quilters—those who wanted to learn to quilt needed to turn to their grandmothers instead of their mothers.
1930	The Depression in the United States caused an interest in quilting again. Not only did families need the warmth, but the U.S. government started a program called the Works Progress Administration (W.P.A.) that provided jobs and encouragement to people who did quilting, weaving, and other arts and crafts. Through the program, many artisans and artists were able to make a living.
1930s	Quilts with scalloped edging become popular.
1939–1945	Patchwork kits were sent over to British prisoners in P.O.W. camps.
1940–1960	Known as the "transitional" period for Amish quilters. Lighter colors and even pastels began to appear. However, their quilts remained in solid colors—no prints.
1960s	The "contemporary" period for Amish quilts. It featured a rediscovery of "traditional" quilt designs, with their strong visual impact. The Amish quilts of today are not so much a functional product as a marketable one.
1970s	Quilting is seen as more of an art form.
1970–1990s	Speed quilting using new tools, like the rotary cutter, becomes popular.

Quilting Terms

Amish Borders	joining borders with a square corner rather than a mitered corner or other border
Appliqué	stitching a fabric cutout on a background fabric
Backing	the bottom layer of your quilt
Bar Tack	zigzagging over a piece of yarn or ribbon, used in machine-tying a quilt
Basting	a long-running stitch used to hold three layers together; it is later removed
Batting	filling that goes between the quilt top and the backing
Bias	a true 45-degree angle on a woven fabric
Binding	a strip of fabric used to enclose the raw edges of all three quilt layers—top, batting, and backing
Block	sometimes called a square; usually fabric sewn together to create a pattern or design
Borders	strips of fabric used to frame your quilt top
Calico	fabric, usually cotton muslin, in which a pattern is repeated in 1-inch squares. In the United Kingdom, the term *calico* refers to muslin without pattern. *The former meaning is used in this book.*
Chain-Stitching	sewing pairs of pattern pieces, one right behind the other, without cutting the thread connecting them—done on a sewing machine
Enlarging Patterns	the pattern pieces in this book do not need to be enlarged; however, if you wish to make, say, the butterfly quilt with larger squares you may want to enlarge the pattern. Trace the pattern pieces on a 1-inch grid, then draw a 1½-inch grid and copy your pattern onto it. This will enlarge your pattern one and a half times.
Fabric Marker	tailor's chalk, a special pen, or other writing implement made just for tracing pattern pieces. *Always test your marker on a piece of fabric to make sure the mark will wash out.*
Finishing	choosing a method to complete the project
Finger-Press	rubbing up and down with your finger and applying pressure at the same time to form a crease

Grain	the direction of the threads in your fabric. *Lengthwise grain runs parallel to the selvage edge; crosswise grain has more stretch than lengthwise grain and runs perpendicular to the selvage edge.*
Grid	evenly spaced horizontal and perpendicular lines
Half-Square Triangle	triangle formed by cutting or folding fabric square in half diagonally (*see Speed Techniques*)
Loft	thickness of the fiber or batting. *In quilting, the higher the loft number, the thicker the batting.*
Mitering	I prefer Amish borders, but many people like mitered borders. *Join two corners at a 45-degree angle.*
Pane	term used in Ireland for a quilt block
Patched Quilt	small pieces of fabric appliquéd on a full-size piece of fabric
Pieced Quilt	small pieces of fabric sewn together to create a pattern
Pivot	a needle on which, in this case, fabric will turn
Pressing	applying a warm iron and steam to fabric to create a smooth, wrinkle-free quilt piece
Quilting	small stitches used to hold all three layers—top, batting, and backing—together
Quilting Pattern	a design used as a model to create your own quilt
Quilt top	the top layer of what will become your coverlet, or quilt
Sashes	pieces of fabric used to frame patchwork or pieced blocks
Seam Allowance	distance between the stitching and the cutting edge of your fabric
Selvage	the finished edges on both sides of a woven fabric
Template	a pattern shape used to trace or cut a design for a pieced or patchwork quilt
Tie points	marks where the pieced top will be tied
Tri-Squares, or Triangle-Squares	the same as a half-square triangle
Tying	a way of holding together three layers of the quilt
Whipstitch	a small overcast stitch

Metric Equivalents

Inches to Millimetres and Centimetres

INCHES	MM	CM	INCHES	CM	INCHES	CM
⅛	3	0.3	9	22.9	30	76.2
¼	6	0.6	10	25.4	31	78.7
⅜	10	1.0	11	27.9	32	81.3
½	13	1.3	12	30.5	33	83.8
⅝	16	1.6	13	33.0	34	86.4
¾	19	1.9	14	35.6	35	88.9
⅞	22	2.2	15	38.1	36	91.4
1	25	2.5	16	40.6	37	94.0
1¼	32	3.2	17	43.2	38	96.5
1½	38	3.8	18	45.7	39	99.1
1¾	44	4.4	19	48.3	40	101.6
2	51	5.1	20	50.8	41	104.1
2½	64	6.4	21	53.3	42	106.7
3	76	7.6	22	55.9	43	109.2
3½	89	8.9	23	58.4	44	111.8
4	102	10.2	24	61.0	45	114.3
4½	114	11.4	25	63.5	46	116.8
5	127	12.7	26	66.0	47	119.4
6	152	15.2	27	68.6	48	121.9
7	178	17.8	28	71.1	49	124.5
8	203	20.3	29	73.7	50	127.0

MM—MILLIMETRES   CM—CENTIMETRES

Yards to Metres and Metres to Yards

YARDS	METRES	YARDS	METRES	YARDS	METRES	YARDS	METRES	YARDS	METRES
⅛	0.11	2⅛	1.94	4⅛	3.77	6⅛	5.60	8⅛	7.43
¼	0.23	2¼	2.06	4¼	3.89	6¼	5.72	8¼	7.54
⅜	0.34	2⅜	2.17	4⅜	4.00	6⅜	5.83	8⅜	7.66
½	0.46	2½	2.29	4½	4.11	6½	5.94	8½	7.77
⅝	0.57	2⅝	2.40	4⅝	4.23	6⅝	6.06	8⅝	7.89
¾	0.69	2¾	2.51	4¾	4.34	6¾	6.17	8¾	8.00
⅞	0.80	2⅞	2.63	4⅞	4.46	6⅞	6.29	8⅞	8.12
1	0.91	3	2.74	5	4.57	7	6.40	9	8.23
1⅛	1.03	3⅛	2.86	5⅛	4.69	7⅛	6.52	9⅛	8.34
1¼	1.14	3¼	2.97	5¼	4.80	7¼	6.63	9¼	8.46
1⅜	1.26	3⅜	3.09	5⅜	4.91	7⅜	6.74	9⅜	8.57
1½	1.37	3½	3.20	5½	5.03	7½	6.86	9½	8.69
1⅝	1.49	3⅝	3.31	5⅝	5.14	7⅝	6.97	9⅝	8.80
1¾	1.60	3¾	3.43	5¾	5.26	7¾	7.09	9¾	8.92
1⅞	1.71	3⅞	3.54	5⅞	5.37	7⅞	7.20	9⅞	9.03
2	1.83	4	3.66	6	5.49	8	7.32	10	9.14

Index

About the Author

Fran Roen describes herself as a busy quilter who spends long Minnesota winters seated at her desk or sewing machine, hiding behind bubble glasses. One by one, she says, she drags her children downstairs to her office/sewing room to ask what they think of her new quilt designs or drawings. The children quickly nod approval and run upstairs, afraid that their mother's crazy love of quilting will rub off.

This is Ms. Roen's third book on speed quilting for Sterling. Her first two books are Country Quilts in a Day and 7-Day Country Quilts. The author has been quilting for more than 20 years and has taught quilting for over 10 years. Ms. Roen has won over 40 ribbons for her quilts and paintings. She comes from a large family and has eight children.